THE PHILOSOPHY OF SAMUEL BECKETT

By the same author

PURSUIT (Autobiography)
THE GARDEN OF EROS
A SAMUEL BECKETT READER (Ed)
A WILLIAM BURROUGHS READER (Ed)
A HENRY MILLER READER (Ed)
THE NOUVEAU ROMAN READER (Ed with John Fletcher)
WHAT'S WRONG, WHAT'S RIGHT? (Poems)

THE PHILOSOPHY OF SAMUEL BECKETT

JOHN CALDER

CALDER PUBLICATIONS
London

RIVERRUN PRESS
New Jersey

CALDER PUBLICATIONS
an imprint of

ALMA BOOKS LTD
3 Castle Yard
Richmond
Surrey TW10 6TF

www.calderpublications.com

ISBN Hardcover 978 0 7145 4284 3
ISBN Paperback 978 0 7145 4283 6

British Library Cataloguing in Publication Data is available
Library of Congress Cataloging in Pulications data is available

Typeset in 10/12pt Palatino by J. W. Arrowsmith Ltd, Bristol
Printed by CreateSpace

ACKNOWLEDGEMENTS

This book can only be dedicated to its subject, whose personality has had a profound influence on my life, just as his writings have dominated my thinking about what life is or should be about. I am extremely grateful to Bill Swainson, a one-time colleague who not only improved the text when copy-editing it, but made valuable suggestions about certain conclusions which I had to rethink. He also insisted on my finding all the sources. A very few are missing because of the ten year gap between writing the book and publishing it, but they are not of great importance.

Sheila O'Leary (now Dillon) carefully retyped the original manuscript and was helpful in many other ways and Laurie Chamberlain put it on disc for the printer. I am grateful to both of them, also to Elena Goodinson who started the latter job which Laurie finished.

There are so many publications about Samuel Beckett that I have limited the works by Samuel Beckett given in the first appendix to those I have used for this study, and only give a short list of further reading for the same reason.

Assuming that no one will want to read this book who does not have a knowledge and interest in the work of its subject, I have not given plots or description of events in Beckett's writings except where necessary to clarify my points. The many references to 'The Trilogy' are of course to the three novels which have been published together at the author's request, namely *Molloy, Malone Dies* and *The Unnamable*.

Contents

1. Preoccupations and Sources   1

2. Philosophy as Fiction: Murphy and Watt   16

3. Man's Inhumanity and The Search for Love   48

4. The Conquest of Time   62

5. The Failure of Art   75

6. Philosophy and Language   85

7. Looking at God   106

8. Prescriptions for Living: Beckett's Ethics   129

End Notes   143

Bibliography   147

Index   149

1

Preoccupations and Sources

Voltaire considered himself to be a novelist, a poet, a dramatist and a writer of opera libretti, but we think of him today largely as a philosopher. The same fate may overtake Samuel Beckett, because what future generations can expect to find in his work is above all an ethical and philosophical message; the novels and plays will increasingly be seen as the wrapping for that message. This will no way detract from the originality and daring of the stage works nor from the power and craftsmanship of the fictions. They were however written for a purpose: to make us face, head-on, the realities of the human condition; and nowhere does he offer us a hopeful message, only a positive attitude and an injunction to face those realities with courage and dignity. Beckett was the last of the great stoics.

Instead of covering ground already well-trodden, I want to concentrate in this short book on the attitudes, the thinking, and the intellectual background of Samuel Beckett the philosopher, and where exegis is necessary—there are many puzzles that have not been solved concerning the meaning of certain episodes and situations in the work—to concentrate on those parables and metaphors that dramatise Beckett's philosophy seen as a whole.

It seems self-evident to me that Beckett is the most significant writer of the twentieth century: he represents the culmination of the achievements of his three most important predecessors, Proust, Kafka, and Joyce. The key elements in their work, Proust's demonstration of the elasticity of time, Kafka's brooding sense of menace, prescient of the horrors to come in his own Germanic and Jewish world, and Joyce's ability to blend myth with daily life through language—all find their synthesis in the literature of Beckett. The twentieth century has been rich in the arts, partly because its eventful history has given artists much material, either to use, illustrate and distort in their work, or from which to escape, as did the major figures of the ivory-tower twenties like T.S Eliot. Yet the three writers I have mentioned, with Beckett as their successor, intellectually dominate that period, standing head and shoulders above a horde of other literary figures most of whom are better known to the public and much more widely read. Proust, Kafka, Joyce and Beckett will, however, be the names that will loom largest when the twentieth century can be seen in perspective.

Beckett in particular has understood his own time as if he were already looking back on it at the time of writing. He has understood its social and military horrors, its criminal wastage of lives and of the planet's resources, its refusal to look at the consequences of selfishness and short-term profit, and he has peered ahead, prophetically—and not very far ahead at that—to a world of want and deprivation, possibly even to the extinction of life on earth. He does not portray such an outcome as necessarily a tragedy, more as an escape from the misery of conscious existence and, in particular, an end to the cruelty of man. This is not expressed without some hesitation and misgivings, because life has so much to offer to some, in particular to those able to appreciate the glories of human achievement in the arts and the great architectural monuments left to us by different periods of civilisation, as well as by the shorter-lived pleasures of the body. Ultimately, however, when weighed in the scales, all these things are very light compared to the great burden of human and animal misery. The enjoyment of power and wealth, available to very few, even the enjoyment of reasonable comfort in times of peace and civilised prosperity, does not come into consideration. These things are unstable, short-lived and belong to those who prefer to be blind to the real world. As with Schopenhauer, Beckett came to the conclusion that life is no blessing and it would be better never to have been born.

Great artistic ages have always been followed by an era of barbarism, during which the arts and the accompanying advances of knowledge are sometimes badly damaged, if not utterly destroyed, or else are absorbed into the new dominant culture that has overwhelmed them. A culture can be conquered by force and become a reluctant possession, as was the case of Greece overcome by Rome, or sometimes only kept alive by small communities of monks or men of culture, hidden away to be rediscovered in the future. Increasing speed of communication from the age of printing onward has made the complete destruction of culture and knowledge much more difficult: the totalitarian regimes of the twentieth century, right and left, have been able to eliminate some individuals and many works of art, but never the culture of which they were a part; knowledge has become too widespread to be lost. The world has shrunk, making most censorship impossible, but not the exercise of brutality and genocide, giving a more sinister meaning to *ars longa, vita brevis*.

Artists can see the horrors that are taking place in the world perfectly well and some of them are doing what little they can to create more awareness in society at large, but many more are giving way to apathy, treating art as an escape from reality, a comfortable, insulated world, metaphorically like the haven that Vladimir and Estragon hope Godot will offer them. That this latter world resembles in many ways an acceptable, non-violent death is not significant, and the relevance of such art produced to the real world can also be questioned. It is the norm of the western world to live as if in a dream, through habit and a disciplined timetable, pushing what is unpleasant outside consciousness. Beckett could not accept membership of that world: he had a compulsion to create his own wounds and rub salt in them. Aesthetically, he needed to suffer pain to intensify his consciousness, and paradoxically there is the desire, expressed in much of his work, to reduce the thresholds of pain and feeling in order to suffer less. In *Proust* Beckett talks of 'the wisdom of all sages from Brahma to Leopardi, the wisdom that consists not in the satisfaction but in the ablation of desire' and quotes the latter:

In noi de cari inganni
non che la speme, il desiderio e spento.[1]

Along with this 'ablation' is the determination to resist the seductions of ambition and to become nothing, to desire nothing, expect nothing and be nothing, along the lines advocated by Arnold Geulincx in his *Ethica*.[2]

Geulincx played an important part in the development of the young Beckett who found a kindred spirit in the writings of this Belgian follower of Descartes. There is however, a significant difference in motivation and by the time he discovered Geulincx, Beckett had lost the Christian faith of the philosophical espouser of poverty and humility. Geulincx was not a well-known name in Trinity and Beckett appears to have come across him more or less by accident in the university library, although he may have been guided by other reading. Geulincx is quoted in *Murphy* (see Chapter 2) and is the source of the first words spoken in *Waiting for Godot*, 'Rien a faire' or 'Nothing to be done'. The essence of his view of the world is that man is a tiny being of no importance in the immensity of God's creation and should conduct himself accordingly.

Meditative philosophy always returns to the same ontological questions: the meaning of existence, the nature of reality, the presence of an immortal soul, the relationship of body to mind, what can be believed and how belief can be tested and proved. Questions about God, on the other hand, mostly belong to theology and are contained within the limits of dogma. Beckett's thinking belongs to the first category, but he was interested both from a literary point of view and from the nostalgia of a religious background in the second. Descartes was a natural starting point for any student of French, as was the theological world of Dante for anyone studying Italian literature. Beckett's first tutor at Trinity College was Dr Arthur Luce, a philosopher who had written much about both Descartes and Bishop Berkeley; these soon became potent influences on Beckett's thinking and writing. But he moved on from general arts studies to learn foreign languages and Thomas Rudmose-Brown, teaching French, and Walter Starkie, Italian , became the principal influences on the formation of his tastes and the direction of his studies. The rationalist world of Descartes, the reflective philosopher *par excellence*, and the imaginative, literary, macabre, and the almost sadistic world of Dante, fused in the mind of the young Samuel Beckett to produce a potent mix. That fusion is apparent in all his work, even in the early novel, *Dream of Fair to Middling Women* which was posthumously published in 1993 and which, like Dante in the Inferno, Beckett had used to settle old scores and satirise his acquaintances.

Beckett's attraction to the philosophical quest for truth would become the background for his most popular novels, popular in the sense that they came nearest to the traditional third-person narrative with plots and episodes that are entertaining as well as instructive to the intelligent, if conventional general reader. But the grotesquerie of Dante is also present in them—and even more unusual Dantesque situations and images were to occur in the works that followed - as well as in his earlier collection of sequential short stories, *More Pricks Than Kicks*, where the hero's name, Belacqua, comes directly out of *Purgatorio*.[3] Belacqua is Beckett's alter ego, reflecting a self-perception that probably chimed with the view his despairing family took of him at the time as an idle layabout. But Beckett always described himself, even to close friends later in life, as not doing anything much in particular even while engaged on his most intensive and significant works, so no one should take that self-perception too seriously. He always seems to have been writing something, poems, fragments, beginnings of stories, novels or essays, but during his early days, and especially before leaving Dublin, he had very little confidence in his own literary abilities. He had no desire to write in any currently acceptable style, and was unsure of the value of his literary experimentations. Into the character of Belacqua he put all his complexes, fears, failings and accident-proneness. Even after *Dream of Fair to Middling Women* and *More Pricks than Kicks*, Belacqua still surfaces occasionally, obliquely, in his writing.

The intellectual proximity of many Christian mystics such as Geulincx to Buddhism is obvious, particularly in the denigration or merging of the individual self into the whole nature of the cosmos. Murphy, who is in search of *nirvana*, is

Beckett's most Buddhist creation, although the concept of the sinking of personal consciousness into a transcendental whole crops up many times. Christian mystics are of course highly suspect to the establishments of all churches, being always on the border of heresy and often beyond it, which is why so many of the medieval thinkers who appealed to Beckett were burnt at the stake. Beckett's reading as a young man was vast but he seldom alluded to it. We can safely assume that he had read or at least knew the ideas of all the major philosophers and of many obscure ones. Certainly, Schopenhauer appealed to him closely and Lance St. John Butler[4] has made a convincing case for the influence of Heidegger, but it is unlikely that the effect on his work of all that he read will ever be known, and in any case it is not of much importance. Beckett took what he needed wherever he found it and was fascinated every time he discovered that his own preoccupations, general frame of thinking and *penchant* for a pessimistic outlook on the world were not peculiar to himself. In his work he quoted widely those with whom he empathised, not because they influenced him, but because they reinforced his convictions. The language, the metaphors, the visual aids and conceptual conceits and inventions which he needed to turn the philosophy of negation, that he shared with many thinkers he had read, into a remarkable new literature that projects a world view to live by, and to die by, he found on his own.

The richness of the whole canon was evident enough when he died at the end of 1989, but with time it is becoming ever richer. It is now possible to view Proust, Kafka and Joyce as one-sided geniuses, and to sum up the essence of their achievement in a few words, but one cannot do this with Beckett. The facets of his work and discoveries are innumerable. He can be read for pure pleasure without going very deeply into meaning, and one can peel off the layers of language and reference—because he refers a great deal—to find ever more riches underneath. It is not necessary to do this to perceive his greatness—most people will find enough truths and insights into their personal predicaments without having to become scholars—but those who take the trouble to look further will be richly rewarded. And, controversially, I do not believe Beckett can really be taught, in the way that I do not believe Beethoven can be either.

The first steps to enjoyment and understanding must be made personally, because Beckett, like Beethoven, appeals in the first instance through atmosphere and emotion. One can guide people to Beckett, but explanations of what he is doing will not work through standard teaching: one reason is that Beckett is never dry; the role of the instinct is more important than imparting a teacher's knowledge, even his discoveries, at second hand. In my opinion, it is a paradox that the most taught modern author is unteachable. What can be conveyed to others is one's own enthusiasm, and guidance can be given to enable the reader or playgoer to make his or her own discoveries. Books about Beckett can be more successful than Beckett-teaching for the simple reason that one is more inclined to read a book about Beckett when one is already fairly familiar with his work. It must also be said that absorption in Beckett's writings, on whatever level, does not necessarily produce the same reaction in every reader. There is so much to be found in them, hidden meanings, references, parallels, the daring with which he launches totally new concepts—these often astonish readers who wonder why they have never thought of something so obvious before—that different readers may draw some of the same information from a text but come to quite different conclusions, all of which can be valid. Beckett the story teller, for example, is rather different from Beckett the philosopher, but usually we get the two together. Sometimes he may get carried away by the momentum of his own creation, so that the text will say something quite different from what he himself believes. When an author invents a character, even a character who invents a philosophy, it does not necessarily follow that the author believes the philosophy of his character, only that he believes his created personality believes it. So when Beckett portrays God, as he often does, he is not saying that he believes in the existence of a God, such as is described by the world's religions, and certainly not that he believes in what that God is saying.

He is simply presenting a popular belief, often satirically, often quite wickedly, and following the natural consequences of that belief to their logical conclusions.

Beckett himself denied that he had any aspirations to be a philosopher or to write about philosophy, saying on one occasion that he could not understand anything philosophers wrote.[5] One can take that for a tactful expression of his indifference to the mass of verbiage in which so many philosophers cloak their essential message. Beckett had the capacity to get to the heart of something, and he also realised that a basic truth is best expressed in simple and elegant language. A key phrase, perhaps a paraphrase, of a philosopher's conclusion or insight, was sufficient for him as a starting point for a novel, a play, even a poem, which would then expand the meaning of the phrase. Had Beckett tried to write direct philosophical treatises they would have been remarkably short, as were his later literary texts.

Nevertheless a definite philosophy emerges from the work and it is not difficult to disentangle it from its wrappings. What must be separated is the myth-making from the admonition. The philosophy is all part of the same whole, and Beckett never preaches directly: what he suggests about the way in which we should conduct our lives is said by presenting situations in which what it means to behave well is quite obvious, usually under the most unfavourable conditions. Life is a patchwork of illusions and delusions and we are shown them even as he explodes them. We see people as they really behave, and recognise them from life. A bully like Pozzo, whose name is at least partly derived from the brand name of an Italian sewer component, is depicted as unpleasant and pompous, but he eventually invites our pity when we see him in distress, and our admiration when we watch him still grimly hanging on to what is left of his dignity. The same is true of Hamm in *Endgame*. To understand is—in most cases— to forgive.

What Beckett makes abundantly clear is that we all have to face the same end, and what may be different is how we manage it. Like T. S. Eliot's phrase 'Birth, copulation and death'[6] summing up human existence, Beckett sees life reduced to three key moments, and the span between birth and death as so short that the two terminal events are virtually the same instant. This is dramatically and effectively brought out many times, notably in Pozzo's final outburst in *Godot* and the French poem in which Beckett writes of living 'the space of a door / that opens and shuts'[7]; in his thirty-second play *Breath*, a life is exactly that long. Only birth and death have real significance. In between lies a pointless existence, a great waste of the magic of creation, a non-event that follows the fusion that has made life: the waiting, the trivia, which we can see as a journey to nowhere or an extended dream; the growing-up, the career or lack of one, the decline.

Success and failure are neither significant nor different, as they lead inevitably to the same end. Success is only a trap, offering a temporary and false security which can crumble away at any time, because of accident, illness or the intervention of others, and it is always harder to fall from a height than if one is already near, or at, the bottom. That is one reason Beckett personally eschewed personal comfort all his life, and never allowed the circumstances of his very real success as a writer to change his thinking, his life or his expectations. His many written statements on the folly of ambition and the irrelevance of failure to anything real are among his most potent and comforting, because they help to remove a major anxiety. There is neither fault nor shame in failure. The cause, more often than not, is accident, just as the situation into which one is born is an accident, part of the chaos and general mess of all existence.

What to many is a source of wonder, the organisation of atoms, molecules, and DNA to form structures that work in observed science (human and other life forms), the systems of survival where everything eats and lives off something else (the balance of nature), the rotation of stars and planets, and, to quote Bertrand Russell, 'the Pythagorean power by which number holds sway above the flux'[8] does not touch Beckett's outlook one whit. He does not share Kant's wonder at the stars that shine above us. In nature he sees only cruelty and pain and states quite clearly that the reason for our existence might simply be to allow pain to exist.[9] The Darwinian principles accepted by science for the animal and vegetable world and by theorists of the political rights for human society, intimating that all the lopping off of the weaker specimens is to strengthen the structure of the race and human progress, is not acceptable to Beckett. He is more interested in the weak than the strong, because it is in his nature to pity and sympathise with the former, not to admire power and success, which is usually acquired at the expense of others. Much of the revolutionary message that lies behind Beckett's practice of turning the fictional world of heroes and villains upside down has never been understood, least of all by the most of the academics who teach him. His equivalents to Shakespeare's Hamlet, Henry V and Richard III are not princes and kings, but the tramps on the street, the undesirables who get pushed out of sight by the police to avoid arousing compassion or guilt in those who see them. It is by understanding what is happening in their minds, concerned primarily with survival and a few small comforts and satisfactions before they die, and in their view of society seen from the bottom, that we can get a grip on the deeper truths of existence, not by studying the relative success of one species over another, or the politics of national power struggles.

We live in a time when political Darwinism, together with the uncontrollable growth of the human population, is leading to a breakdown of the humane and social values which have been built slowly over centuries. These values in the developed countries support the civilisations of many cultures, and in less developed countries as well. While not perfect, they appeared to be slowly leading to a future society based on justice, liberty and conviviality, as well as a social scale, which, while not offering equality, did seem to be taxing the richest to help support the poorest. That liberal society to which the Victorian thinkers looked forward, confident that it would soon rule the earth, was destroyed by the greed of nations and individuals, by renascent nationalism and tribalism, and the values of, first the fascist dictators, then, after the golden but deceptive Sixties (the heyday of Beckett's advanced creativity and his acceptance by the intelligentsia), the return of naked power-lust and greed, symbolised and lead by Thatcher, Marcos, Nixon and their like. They did not represent a tyranny in political terms; they were simply indifferent to the plight of the victims of the society they represented, and feudal in their thinking. Those who fall below the poverty line became non-citizens, of no importance and to be denied any succour from the state in terms of shelter, medical care or the ability to continue living other than as wild animals. A clochard stabbed Beckett in the street in Paris in the Thirties, and was unable to give any reason for his act. But that Beckett understood well enough the mind of such a person is clear in his portrayal of Molloy, aware of how he is seen by those with houses to live in and food to eat, who regard anything that lives outside their comfortable circumstances as prey for an enjoyable hunt.[10] Tyranny is not a part of the indifferent society of feudal capitalism. It belongs to the totalitarian world, with which capitalism is nevertheless always linked. The crudities of the regime of a Gadafi or a Saddam Hussein are intended to form a society without dissent, ruled from above in the interests of the rulers, but it is also capable of benign generosity towards all strata in exchange for unquestioning loyalty, often with good social programmes, adequate health care and the external features of a welfare state. Beckett, by implication, links capitalist neglect with the power of tyrants, and in doing so is comically dismissive of all welfare activities.

Although Beckett had the reputation, except in Eastern Europe during the Sixties and Seventies, of being non-political—he was far too aware of the larger issues to be willing to fritter away the value of his signature on manifestoes that would be signed by all the usual names, and he often felt that, as a guest in France, he had no right to comment on French affairs—he was in fact intensely political in the sense of being always aware of what was happening in the world and thinking about it. He saw few films, but one he did see was *Mondo Cane*, which portrayed as a documentary the human cruelty, much of it casual, that one camera team could witness, around the world, with more than a suspicion that some of it was instigated by those who made the film. Just as he would not allow himself, at a time when his success was bringing in a considerable royalty income, to enjoy the comforts that belong to a successful writer, and lived as simply as a monk,[11] he also had a compulsion to inflict more suffering on himself by living in the proximity of suffering. His flat on the Boulevard St Jacques overlooked, from its back windows, the Santé prison. He knew its geography perfectly and exactly where the guillotine was situated before France abolished capital punishment. When staying with him at Ussy, his cottage in the country, I went for a walk with him one fine morning. Once outside his gate he declined to go in one direction rather than another: 'The slaughter house is down there!' The only manifesto that he ever signed, until late in his life, was for the humane slaughtering of animals, not a political issue in France, where some people believe that meat tastes better if the animal dies in panic and pain.

Ethics are indivisible from politics, which is why I believe that an ethical philosopher—which is what in essence he is—cannot avoid being seen in political terms. But Beckett was always above party and ideology, and politically above country as well. He loved France, for its culture, its tolerance, its atmosphere, its appreciation of life, and in spite of his asceticism and refusal to lead a normal comfortable existence, for its food, wine, beautiful buildings, history and sensual pleasures. But he enjoyed these things only on a day to day basis: to enjoy today is not to expect to enjoy tomorrow, or even to be alive tomorrow. His famous riposte, during a visit to Lords with Harold Hobson to watch cricket, on hearing Hobson say, 'It's a day to make you feel happy to be alive,' was 'I wouldn't go so far as that!' Two or three years before he died, I was walking through Montparnasse with him and it being a fine morning, remarked, 'What a beautiful day!' His instant reply was 'So far.'

Living for the day, because there is no certain future, explains one paradox of the man who denied himself nearly every comfort, but he could appreciate a good meal in a good restaurant, enjoyed and knew his wines, liked the company of friends and could with discrimination look at a painting, listen to and play music, and sink himself into literary creation, which however painful he might protest he found it, was, as he knew well, his *raison d'être*. Every artist is tortured by the experience of creating art, but it is also his escape from the outside world, and from worry, pain, and both company and solitude.

Nobody ever knew when Beckett was working; he always claimed not to be. He certainly produced more when alone in the country than when in town, because in Paris it was appointments with people who wanted to meet him, or with friends, or with theatres and publishers, that occupied him. But his output proves his industry, especially when one realises the hours of revision that went into every sentence, the reworkings, new starts, the cuts, and the condensations, to say nothing of the immense time that went into translating his own work! No writer can ever have been more meticulous. But he was equally conscientious about answering letters, even those that were sent to him just to get his signature on a reply, and in dealing with everyday matters. Beckett's *emploi du temps* is unfathomable. Like Sir Walter Scott, he was immensely industrious, but always seemed to have time for everyone else, without seeming hurried. He was so punctilious that one could literally set one's watch by the second of his arrival. He was impatient with others who were late, except where he knew from experience that it was so ingrained in their habits that he must always expect a certain delay, and he usually knew how late someone was likely to be, because latecomers tend to be punctual in their lateness.

Beckett realised that life is a total accident, but whereas others considered themselves supremely lucky to be fathered by the fusion of one sperm in billions that found one egg in millions, Beckett felt the opposite. That tiny chance of life is a supreme disaster, because even if one is born into fortunate circumstances, lives in a period of peace in a prosperous civilisation, in a part of the world where such things are possible, one still has to face the lifelong certainty that one will die at the end; nothing is certain during that lifetime, nor can one know how or when one will die.

Religion for those who can accept its comforts is a palliative, but it was one that a thinking man of honesty and courage such as Beckett could not accept. He had thought out all the illogicalities of religion and, in private, because he wisely never declared himself in public, he made it clear that he believed in no afterlife and in no deity interested in mankind.

Was he a theist like Voltaire? I think not: his fictional deities, particularly as portrayed in the Moran section of *Molloy*, where he ridicules Christianity (note that Moran is a Catholic, not an adherent of the Protestant faith, culture and ethic in which Beckett was bought up), and in *Ill Seen Ill Said*, where God is speaking and trying to undo his own handiwork, are creations from his own imagination of theology, not of metaphysics, nor even of philosophy. The philosophy of Beckett is not always or necessarily a part of my examination of these texts, although obliquely Beckett's deeply felt convictions are behind them, revolutionary and deeply destructive of orthodox Christianity, and Judaism as well. They are part of the author's sense of loss, of the world of belief that disappeared with his childhood and growing critical intelligence. Like Prince Siddhartha, Beckett grew up in a world where he was allowed to see no evil, no suffering. When he realised its overwhelming presence, he had to react, and did so by becoming a writer whose objective, however undeliberate and instinctive, was not to heal—he knew that was impossible—but to offer some solace, a helping hand. One's own suffering is diminished when one looks at the sufferings of others. Beckett knew from experience and from deep thought, partly connected with his years of hiding in Roussillon during the war, partly from the time he believed he was going to die from a tumour in his cheek, what it was to live in the constant expectation of death.

His early work already suggests a powerful philosophical mind. But it was the years from 1947 to 1949, lived almost entirely in solitude that turned him into both a Descartes and a Dante, the one writer who made it possible, not only to understand the underlying spirit of man in the twentieth century, but of all the time before it, as if all existence were but one interrupted nightmare in the history of time.

2

Philosophy as Fiction: *Murphy* and *Watt*

In drama, language cannot escape from the need to be colloquial. It imposes a rhetoric on the text, and also the need to elevate that rhetoric above the exchange of spoken dialogue, which however poetic it may be, cannot avoid a certain flatness. If the exchange of views, observations, attitudes and differences brought out by the actors are to be understood by the audience, everyday reality must occupy part of the stage business, acting as a hitching-post. Longer speeches can soar above that flatness and contrast with it; in every play we recognise highlights, and in great plays we are inclined to remember lines and phrases, sometimes whole monologues, because they have made a strong impression on us.

Drama gives wonderful opportunities to the writer to play on the audience's emotions, excite the intellect, and, occasionally, to put over his views on political, moral, or philosophical issues. Although we are aware of language in drama, language is not necessarily the most important element in the construction of the play: if anything it limits the playwright, while it encourages the novelist or essayist to expand its possibilities. The presence of a visual and an auditory quality in spoken drama makes language a partner in the art, not the whole art itself. Beckett, if he believed in anything, believed in language: '. . . words have been my only loves, not many.'[12] He always felt that he was primarily a novelist and that his involvement in the theatre, which he welcomed for its conviviality and opportunity to work creatively with others, in contrast to being alone in a room, was largely an accident. He reputedly said to Deirdre Bair: 'the best possible play is one in which there are no actors, only the text. I am trying to find a way to write one.' He did of course succeed with *Breath*. However Beckett's *caveats*, made in conversation, often depended on his mood, and many of them should not be taken too seriously.

Beckett's feelings about language are forcefully expressed in a letter he wrote in 1937 to a German friend, Axel Kaun, about whom nothing is later known and who may well have perished in Hitler's holocaust. Beckett had at that time written three works of fiction, a short book on Proust, much poetry, and was emerging from the overwhelming influence of Joyce. He had in fact found his own voice, although his wartime experiences would change both its tone and its purpose in the next decade. He was struggling with language in the sense that he was still unsure of how to tame it to express what he wanted, perplexed by the many ways that language becomes a living force of its own that can dictate the content that floats on it, and have the capacity to hide as much as it reveals.

In his letter to Kaun, written in a German that was adequate but not perfect, and is here translated by Martin Esslin;[13] he says:

> It is indeed becoming more and more difficult, even senseless, for me to write an official English. And more and more my own language appears to me like a veil that must be torn apart in order to get at the things (or the nothingness) behind it. Grammar and style, to me they seem to have become as irrelevant as a Victorian bathing suit or the imperturbability of a true gentleman. A mask. Let us hope the time will come, thank God that in certain circles it has already come, when language is most efficiently used where it is being most efficiently misused. As we cannot eliminate language all at once, we should at least leave nothing undone that might contribute to its falling into disrepute. To bore one hole after another in it, until what lurks behind it—be it something or nothing—begins to seep through; I cannot imagine a higher goal for a writer today.

He goes on to comment that literature appears to have remained behind 'in the old lazy ways', whereas music and painting had moved on to new forms and discoveries. His problems at the time revolved around prose writing, and in particular, the novel. Although he had dabbled with writing a play, he had not made much progress; that was to come after the war. In front of him he had the work of Joyce, not just *Ulysses* but *Finnegan's Wake* as well, like an insurmountable wall, blocking all progress. Much of his first novel, *Dream of Fair to Middling Women*, is pure Joyce, but towards the end of it he largely escapes from the master's mantle. In *More Pricks than Kicks* he had developed his caustic humour to an art, found a readable style that made more demands on the reader's literary knowledge than on his ability to concentrate, but was publishable according to the perception of the publisher. His postwar disdain of *More Pricks than Kicks* ('that old shit')[14] probably stems as much from his later regretting the personal and autobiographical nature of the work as from any rejection of a style that he had by then long abandoned. But although disliking it, he eventually agreed to republication in 1970 after two cyclostyled editions for scholars, limited to a hundred each, had appeared some years earlier. He never tried to disown *Murphy* although it has many of the same autobiographical factors, and was equally 'readable', because he knew that he had succeeded there in writing a work that accurately presented the intellectual and philosophical problems that had preoccupied him since reading Descartes, and he had by then escaped the undergraduate mannerisms that were still present in the earlier work. Published in 1938, only a very few copies survived the London blitz, after poor sales. It was published in the USA in 1957 and reissued in the UK in 1963.

Murphy is largely about escape. How to escape the prison of the body, how to get away from the gravity of the world with all its problems and distractions and not least its human entanglements. In *Murphy* Beckett develops a number of themes and preoccupations, many of them visual, that continue cropping up in his later work. In a short Chapter Six, he gives us a description of Murphy's mind. Murphy is seeking *nirvana*, escape into transcendental meditation, and manages to achieve this, or at least approach a peace of mind, by binding himself to a rocking chair (described in Chapter One), naked, where the tight bonds almost stop him from breathing, barely aware of the outside world with its street sounds and ringing telephones, free in his mind from his body. Only when the body is appeased, i.e. free from sensation, can he come alive in his mind and have the pleasure of free, floating thought, and feel himself on his way to Buddhist meditation, which Murphy, going through different stages of escape, calls the Attunement.

The dualism that emerges increasingly in Beckett's work from the time of *Murphy* takes many forms: the contrast of mind and body, of darkness and light, of success and failure, of power and weakness, rich and poor, heat and cold, usually seen as poles of existence, as also birth and death. Time, although visualised as linear, broken by calendar events, holidays, seasons and interruptions, is also seen as a circle, just as the universe is conceived as circular and it is therefore an entrapment. In a sense linear and circular time, although not necessarily contradictory, are also a dualism. Murphy's mind is also circular, a hollow sphere, at its best when hermetically closed to the universe without. But everything without it is, as Murphy visualises it, also within. In other words, the stoic mind does not need the outside world, it can create everything it needs within its own hollow sphere. Beckett here is cleverly airing the thinking of the classic philosophers of the Enlightenment and their followers, with subtle side glances back to the Greek stoics. It refers in the first place to Descartes for whom the dualism is between thinking substance (which can also be defined in the context of his own theological age as soul) and matter, that is to say the body and the whole world outside the individual mind. For John Locke the knowledge we have in our mind may well come from the outside world and consist of what we ourselves have chosen, but what is important is the 'idea' of it—the whole outside world and what we have chosen to imprison of our knowledge of it inside our minds. But there is a two-way traffic nevertheless, and while the idea may be the most important factor, the material world is always present and real. Bishop Berkeley, refuting Locke, sees only the mind as important: the outside world is contained within it, was created by it, and is of no importance except as a product of that mind. Hume cannot accept Berkeley's idealism. What we know, we know from experience; all knowledge is questionable, all thought may be illusory.

Hume is an intellectual ancestor of the *nouveau roman*, which developed in tandem with Beckett's post war period. Many critics think, mistakenly I believe, that Beckett's novels and those of his French contemporaries, like Robbe-Grillet, are all of the same school. There are many points of similarity, stemming from the relationship of both to surrealism, Joyce, and the avant-garde of the Twenties and Thirties, seeing truth as arbitrary and the mind as an undeveloped organ to be freed from the constraints of logic and rationalism, but that is as far as it goes. Beckett knew the Surrealists well, and he borrowed a few ideas from them, but he always stayed outside the movement; and any similarities with the *nouveau roman* are only superficial.

Beckett was not really interested in playing games in literature (although there is a playfulness that occasionally lightens some of his most important literary work), but in conveying his vision of the world. Philosophy to him was not so much something to be investigated—he had made his mind up early what philosophy attracted him and he returned frequently to those kindred spirits who had thought what he now thought—as subject matter to be illustrated, sometimes mocked, in the novels. In the plays philosophy is discussed and its concepts become the property of many of his characters, but he does not use philosophical ideas to be given human form on the stage. The nature of dramatic dialogue was both a hindrance to his doing so and an opportunity simply to use his characters to speculate or discuss philosophical concepts, not to embody them.

On the other hand, the mind-body conflict, the nature of perceived reality, and the ability of the mind to create a whole universe within its own limitations, seemed to offer rich material for the kind of novel he wanted to write once he had begun to move away from his own experience as a reading and thinking student, whose own life and interests offered many opportunities for satire and interpretation while the lives of his acquaintances offered a similar potential. From

Hume the next step is, of course, Kant. Kant also saw the world in dualistic terms, as the coexistence of the real outside world (the thing in itself) and the world of appearances. For Kant, the mind, perceiving the world, is also part of that world perceived, and is therefore real; the world of phenomena, which we never really understand, but investigate, is the world of shadows: it is, he might have said, also the world of science. But Beckett, for emotional reasons, basically rejects Kant: 'This did not involve Murphy in the idealist tar. There was the mental fact and there was the physical fact, equally real if not equally pleasant.'[15]Beckett does not, like Robbe-Grillet, argue that as every mind is different and has different perceptions and logical processes, it therefore follows that there can be no objective reality. Beckett is only interested in one mind at a time, the mind of a particular hero, and what is real to him is all that matters. Philosophers, looking for truth through their own thought processes, do not tend to pit their own idea of reality against another's as much as to create a synthesis whereby previous thought is contained in their own, which is why we see the history of philosophy, even more than the history of literature, as a chain, usually a single one, because philosophers, just as scientists, must usually be more international in their awareness of what is going on elsewhere. Many writers know little outside the national tradition in which they write, and if their work is often paralleled by that of their contemporaries elsewhere, it is because the *Zeitgeist* presents them with the same images and subject matter.

Nevertheless, Kant is still present in Murphy's self-perception. 'He distinguished between ... that of which he had both mental and physical experience (the thing in itself) and that of which he had mental experience only'[16] (Kant's *a priori* world of phenomena, i.e. being beyond proof or experience).

In Murphy's mind, which however much he might want to achieve *nirvana* or total oblivion to the outside world still seems to be on a fairly high level of waking consciousness, we come across another visual concept which is repeated many times in Beckett's later writings: it is the image of hollow space, a cavity like the inside of the skull, in which the mind resides, but is subject to a changing light going from brightness to gloom to darkness. Later, in such texts as *Imagination Dead Imagine*, this circular movement of light, which of course returns by stages to its initial brightness, is accompanied by a similar variation of heat and cold, like the external world in the day and at night. And the mind is replaced by crouching, imprisoned human figures, so that the mind really contains what is outside it.

The three stages of light in *Murphy* are accompanied by different mental activities. Brightness or 'light' is accompanied intellectually by daydreams in which the protagonist imagines what he wants to imagine, revenge on enemies, voyeuristic sex, the reverse of whatever has occurred in life that is unpleasant. The half light is the condition for contemplation, a pure pleasure, very different, and freed from the emotional, perhaps too exciting, reveries of the full light. The complete dark is akin to hell—we can take it that Beckett was certainly thinking of Dante's three afterworlds here—consisting of commotion and upset, 'nothing but forms becoming and crumbling into the fragments of a new becoming, without love or hate or any intelligible principle of change ... Here he was free, but a mote in the dark of absolute freedom ... '.[17]

Interestingly it is the purgatory, or middle state, which is the pleasant one, the world inhabited by Dante's Belacqua, who simply wanted to relax and think, whose name Beckett used as the hero of his first two fictional works. In the middle state Murphy is Belacqua. But here Beckett already prefigures the revelation that would be described later in *Krapp's Last Tape* of his vocation to seek out the dark side of life (see Chapter Five), rather than to allow himself even the pleasures of the intellect. Murphy moves towards his calvary like a penitent:

> Thus as his body set him free more and more in his mind, he took to spending less and less time in the light, spitting at the breakers of the world; and less in the half light, where the choice of bliss introduced an element of effort; and more and more and more in the dark, in the will-lessness, a mote in its absolute freedom.[18]

Note the twice repeated 'and more' and the final mention of 'a mote', signifying his desire to be small and insignificant, even to disappear altogether, another Beckettian Geulincx-like conceit, close to Kafka's world and the self-abnegation and masochism which seems to be common to most great writers. Kafka turned his hero into a beetle in '*Metamorphosis.*' Beckett might even have considered that fate too good.

Beckett's purpose in *Murphy* and in *Watt* is to describe philosophy rather than to make it. He follows the reasoning of the philosophers he knows, but is little interested in the arguments between them, nor the history by which one system of thought replaces another or augments it. A concept is either congenial and useful to him, or it is not. The positivists leave him cold, not because he questions what they have to say; he just cannot warm to it. As in his *Duthuit Dialogues*, he allows himself to be drawn into argument and to be defeated, retiring silent and unrepentant. Because what matters to him is not so much what man perceives and believes as his condition itself: understanding the laws of physics and our genetic structure is very interesting, but it does not change man's destiny, he will die, each as an individual, taking his knowledge with him. The acquisition of knowledge is simply a way of passing time while we wait to die. As such it is valid: Beckett's characters have a number of ways of passing their time, much of it to do with mathematical calculation which interested the author very much; he once spent much time working out problems, ruminating on conundrums, rather as he did crossword puzzles—to pass the time. As he puts it in his late masterpiece, *Company*, 'Simple sums you find a help in times of trouble. A haven ... Even still in the timeless dark you find figures a comfort.'[19] Such mental exercises keep darker thoughts at bay for a while, so that even the most useless and artificial calculations, like the circulation of sucking stones in *Molloy* and the provision of food for the dog in *Watt* who is to receive Mr Knott's leftovers in all the possible combinations of circumstances, have their purpose, to avert or delay the very awareness that lies behind the writer's obligation to write, which in its turn is to make it more difficult to avoid facing awareness. Kant liked mathematics because they gave discipline to time and space, two of Beckett's principal pre-occupations, and he uses mathematics in his fictional systems to do the same, subsequently destroying their relevance as he deflates them. Even in his most serious moments, Beckett is inclined to mock and make fun of the process of thinking itself and to satirise the philosophies that result from that thinking.

Beckett's penchant for dualism is perhaps stronger in *Murphy* than elsewhere, and as he moved away from the philosophical novel after *Mercier and Camier* and more towards metaphor and parable, the use of this dualism is less obvious. But it is still there in the later work and is particularly evident in his careful and equal division of light and darkness in his manichean play *Krapp's Last Tape*. Manicheism is the religion of dualism. Although his study of Descartes and his awareness of the work of Descartes' followers, Geulincx and Malebranche, to both of whom he refers frequently in his work, set off his interest in investigating dualistic concepts of the mind-body relationship, there is so much dualism in Beckett's background and upbringing, and the Irish world in which he grew up with its Catholic-Protestant divide, its Anglo-Nationalist adversarial politics, and with its class divisions as well, that his cultural manicheism is not surprising. 'Humanity is a well with two buckets,' he says in the *Trilogy*.[20] Characters in his best-known plays tend to be in pairs, Vladimir and Estragon, Pozzo and Lucky, Hamm and Clov, Nagg and Nell, Winnie and Willie, but this is not on the whole true of the novels where it is the characters themselves who are dualistic.

The message that emerges from *Murphy*, and from Beckett's earlier book on Proust, is that the world is an unpleasant place from which escape is desirable. Proust, a snob who envied and wanted desperately to be part of aristocratic smart French society, nevertheless retreated into comfortable solitude and his own mind in order to be able to write his masterpiece, which in many ways is a study of mental time. All of Beckett's *alter ego* characters are also in a sense Adam, the first man. And Adam has brought to man the curse of original sin.

Beckett is in no doubt as to what original sin consists of today: it is 'the sin of having been born'.[21] It follows that to be the first mover in anything is to carry a curse, which is why inaction is preferred to action. In a later chapter I shall look at Beckett's attitude in his writing to the first mover of all: God.

Schopenhauer, one of the most potent influences on Beckett, felt much the same way about the curse of being born. It is the human will that for him is the prime mover towards action, and the human will is evil, leading mankind to evil deeds and the perpetuation through procreation of more evil. Among nineteenth-century philosophers Schopenhauer was almost unique in not believing that the human race was moving towards Utopia and that a time of peace, justice, progress and human happiness lay ahead. Although Beckett was born at exactly the right time to realise the hollowness of that dream—he was twelve when the first world war ended, and that war was the event that made thinking people realise that greed and stupidity were far more powerful forces in the advance of history than rationalism and good intentions—it is unlikely that the war played that big a part in his subsequent attitudes or, for that matter even Irish politics, which were then at fever heat. It was the result of his reading at Trinity, and the heritage of Christian dogma from his school days (its most potent image being that of the crucifixion), and his own natural inclination, that gave him the predilection to pessimism and the desire to escape from the world. Belacqua, mildly condemned by Dante, is not at all condemned by Beckett: he is not a first mover, and therefore can do no harm.

In his chess game with Mr Endon inside the mental home where he has finally taken a job, having resisted work until that point in the novel, Murphy is forced to make the first chess move, thus once again imitating Adam and inheriting his curse. Although the patients in the Magdalen Mental Mercyseat believe themselves to be in a form of prison and the psychiatrists speak of them as being in exile, for Murphy they are in a sanctuary. In the asylum he has a chance to study the mental world and its schizophrenia at first hand, but he is usually disappointed in the inability of the patients to appreciate their luck at having escaped, even temporarily, from the outside world. One patient however is up to expectation, Mr Endon (his name means 'within' in Greek) is perfectly contented, lives entirely in his mind, and cannot be persuaded to take any initiative whatsoever. When confronted with the chess board, Mr Endon will not make a move, forcing Murphy to do so. Moving his white pawn to King's fourth, one of the commonest opening gambits (the subsequent cause of all White's difficulties, as Beckett points out in a series of commentaries on the match), Murphy then has to leave to do his nightly rounds, returning every ten minutes for the next move, but the game is hindered by Mr Endon's great reluctance to move at all, forcing Murphy finally to imitate every move that black makes in order to make Endon move again, and after forty-three moves, Mr Endon's pieces having hopped into all the available spaces and back again, the board is as it was at the beginning except for the two opening pawns that cannot of course be withdrawn. Mr Endon at one point was in a position to check the king, but did not do so, thereby avoiding a victory which Murphy was willing to give him. Murphy had intended to imitate the freedom of the patients to live entirely in their own minds, but his duties, and the non-cooperation of the patients frustrate him.

The barriers to a contemplative life are obvious, and they are well illustrated in the novel. First there are the needs of the flesh: hunger, lust, a place to sleep. Money is necessary for all these things and Murphy's problem is to seek *nirvana* while avoiding work and still finding ways to live. Celia, whom he loves and who loves him, earns her living as a prostitute, but is willing to desist if Murphy will work, but Murphy, whose life apart from meditation is ruled by his horoscope, will only work when the omens are right, not that he has any desire to work at all. The asylum is the work he eventually finds as a male nurse, but it leads to his death: the gas has not been turned off, he is bound in his rocking chair, moving to *nirvana*, but also to death.

Death has of course to be the ultimate escape for all of us.

Every attempt to escape life other than by death is doomed to be frustrated, which is perhaps the main message of *Murphy*. But Beckett's characters continue to seek ways to escape in later fictions and plays. Krapp escapes through the Proustian past, reliving his memories with the aid of a tape recorder on which he has recorded his thoughts every birthday up to the present one, his sixty-ninth: it is an ominous date because he only expects to live to the biblical seventy. But escape is never divorced from pain. The ending passage of *How It Is*, as well as those of the earlier *The Unnamable*, contain the death agonies, but not quite the deaths of the narrators, both breathless, one struggling to crawl while being pulled down by a sea of mud, the other trying to shut out the encroaching silence. There is no dignity in this panic, but the last words nevertheless accept the unavoidable and are even hopeful. *The Unnamable* ends with 'I'll go on.' This can be read as both a hope that there may be a future or that there will be a memory of that existence which is ending. But this facing the end is the subject matter of a later chapter. It is in these moments when the end is near, but has not yet quite arrived, that we realise the significance of Beckett's statement, that the key word in his writing is 'Perhaps'.[22]

In *Murphy* Beckett succeeded in writing a quirky picaresque novel that will be seen in time as belonging to the bohemian literature of the Thirties, a tradition that is less well known than the novels that portrayed the life of the upper classes (Evelyn Waugh, for example), or the committed depression literature about social problems and the dangers of fascism (George Orwell and John Steinbeck). Ultimately *Murphy* demonstrates that however desirable it might be to make the mind body-proof, and the body mind-proof, this can only occasionally be possible; interruptions from one to the other are inevitable. But it launched Beckett on the path of the philosophical novel and in its stylistic innovations it also pointed the way forward beyond Joyce to a form of fiction where the style and the subject matter would become more part of each other. But the war was to intervene, launching Beckett on a new path. Amazingly, his next novel *Watt*, written in hiding at Roussillon between the end of 1942 and 1945, although one can see traces of his wartime experiences in it, is still in the field of the philosophical novel, not of metaphor. So is *Mercier and Camier*, its successor, written in French. *Watt* is Beckett's longest novel, and is still strongly Irish in its background, in every way a philosophical successor to *Murphy*. It is possible that the great leap, during his immuration in solitude from 1947 to 1949 with the writing of *Molloy*, first part of the trilogy, was more the result of his expectation to die from cancer than his wartime experiences.

Whereas *Murphy* is largely about the outer world of appearances, *Watt* is mainly concerned with an inner world and, while also being entertaining and containing much comedy like its predecessor, it embodies different philosophical concepts that interested Beckett, and to which he gives human shapes. The Beckett character here, like Belacqua and Murphy in the past, is Watt, the protagonist, who enters the service of a Mr Knott. We know that all Beckett's character names have a significance. Mr Knott is quite possibly God, and it is not difficult to think of God as being a knot that mankind has always tried to untie or may be untieable unless an Alexander comes along. The Letter 'G' in Beckett usually has some God-like resonance. He has said that Godot is not God but many critics have felt that the play makes much so more sense if he is, and God is the first syllable of Godot. Let us remember too that it was Gideon who tied the knot that could not be unraveled. In a later chapter I shall look at the significance in the names in Molloy, of which Gaber is not only one, but one which seems to have some celestial association. These are all 'G's. But of course the question also arises that God may not be God, the kind of speculation that would easily enter Beckett's mind. The significance of the names is in any case of no real importance at this point, but I shall examine them again in a later chapter.

Watt's attempt to find out as much as possible about Mr Knott might be interpreted, in part, as mankind's search for the nature and the existence of God. Mr Knott hides himself, but he wants his household to know that he exists; *esse est percipi*, Bishop Berkeley's famous phrase, which Beckett made the subject of *Film* in the Sixties, is part of Berkeley's proof of God, but to be perceived is so important an element in all the author's work that more space will be devoted to it later. Mr Knott at one point reveals his face to Watt, presumably as a parody of God revealing his face to Moses. The biblical references all point to Knott's God-like status, but always in the spirit of parody. Beckett extended himself in this novel. He poured into it his perception of the human condition, of his relationship to nature, and all his disgust with the business of living in an unfriendly world, and making it worse. In his description of the Lynch family, where everyone is crippled, disabled, unsightly, or suffering from some terrible ailment, he describes the miserable of the earth, endlessly multiplying and producing more unhealthy, miserable and disabled members of the species, whose only significant activity is to inflict their situation on new generations. In Arsene's famous 'short statement', we get a long monologue of disgust. Arsene is the former servant of Mr Knott who is replaced by Watt. Before leaving he delivers himself of his bile, a sour look at the world, filled with much philosophical comment, with analyses of human problems and containing some of Beckett's most quotable lines, extremely comic in their equally extreme condemnation of both the human world and the natural world of which it is a part. Man's only escape from his suffering and tragedy, Arsene tells us, is through the laugh: the bitter, the hollow and the mirthless.

> The bitter laugh laughs at that which is not good, it is the ethical laugh. The hollow laugh laughs at that which is not true, it is the intellectual laugh . . . But the mirthless laugh is the dianoetic laugh . . . the laugh of laughs, the *risus purus*, the laugh laughing at the laugh . . . at that which is unhappy.[23]

In the first part of *Mirlitonnades*, a group of short, aphoristic poems, which were usually written originally on the back of beer mats or scraps of paper while sitting in cafés, Beckett returns, many years later, to the risus purus:

en face
le pire
Jusqu'a ce
qu'il fasse rire[24]

It is the moment when there is no escape, no solution, no hope, but only the ability left to laugh, mirthlessly, at the whole absurdity of everything, at the cosmic, unfeeling, uncaring, unknowing universe. Yiddish humour is no stranger to the dianoetic laugh, because the Jewish experience, although relieved by an unrealistic optimism, lies very close to Beckett's world. Life is a mess, and in *Watt* Beckett gets off his chest all his natural disgust with everything he has witnessed in the world. It is the author at his most emotional, for once not hiding behind his characters, his own disgust with the human functions of birth, sexual activity, procreation, eating and eliminating the detritus of what one has eaten, of the nursing of babies, the eating of other animals, all the forms of physical and mental torture that are regularly practised and are so popular with our species, the killings and massacres, and of course the dyings. Beckett like everyone else could not escape from bodily functions, but he avoided them as best he could; his preference for solitude had as much to do with his asceticism as with his need to be alone to write. He could distance himself enough to perceive the whole void of existence in a void of nothingness, the *néant* of Sartre and the existentialists, and the negative *Dasein* of Heidegger. The writer who can do this becomes in a sense God himself, because he takes on God's vision and ability to look, unblinkingly, at the whole mess of the world. Ionesco, in one of his most important dramatic moments, has his character, Béranger, do this in *Le Pieton de l'aire (A Stroll in the Air)*. Béranger, having suddenly acquired the ability to jump to a great height and look down, like an astronaut, on the earth, sees all the misery, wars, massacres, persecutions, beneath him. It is God's vision.

Beckett had such a vision from the beginning, and it was impossible for him to push it out of his consciousness. He had to isolate himself, both to control his anger and disgust, and to build an outlook, that while refusing to accept the unacceptable, made it possible for him to put something in the place of total negation. There was never a question of giving up, of ceasing to struggle. To God, to nature, to the panaceas of society as much as to tyranny, there is only one course of action: defiance. Beckett cast himself as Prometheus and was willing, in his mental torment, to share his fate.

It is humour that relieves the shocking and disgusting parts of *Watt*, but the humour of despair, the mirthless laugh, the laugh at that which is unhappy. The other relief is, of course, immersion in the mind, which is represented in the large philosophical content of the novel. But Arsene's speech is in a sense also the beginning of Beckett's dramatic career. It is a long first person monologue, the first of many that would follow in the *Trilogy*, the *Texts for Nothing*, the plays and elsewhere. It is Beckett speaking out loud, pouring a world view into a great rush of words. Arsene hardly ever pauses for breath and there are few full stops in his 'short statement'. It is like a prolonged fart, which might account for the speakers name.

With Arsene gone, Watt goes about his job, speculating about his master, Mr Knott who leaves traces of his presence everywhere, but is never seen. The situation that arises from his riches, and willingness to be charitable, leads to endless complications and, inevitably, instead of reducing the misery without, increases it. Mr Knott only eats a single dish twice a day, a pottage made out of mixing together every imaginable food, and every imaginable drink, and every imaginable medicine, boiled together for hours and served cold. The remains must be given to a hungry dog by Mr Knott's orders, if there are any remains, and there seldom are. The immense complications of ensuring that there is always a starving dog available to eat the leftovers if there are any, and someone to look after the dog, and someone always available to replace the man in case of need, and for another dog always to be available to replace the currently to be fed famished dog, take up many pages and are extremely funny, but behind the comedy lies a clear-eyed vision of the waste of most human endeavour, social planning and attempts to do good, and a cruel picture of the *de facto* cruelty of mankind whether deliberate or not. It can also be seen as God's inept management of the world.

Watt's philosophical speculations take a classical shape that go back to Aristotle and all the theories of reality present in Greek philosophical attempts to describe what is real and proveable and what is unreal and speculative. Watt's extreme literalism is a parody of Descartes' unwillingness to accept anything until he could prove it, and his final reliance on the mind as the only possible judge of reality. There is no place in Beckett's world, or at least in the world of his thinking creations, for the old schoolboy adage that 'all angles that look equal are equal'. Watt looks at a pot, but cannot convince himself that it really is a pot. The more we look at something that appears to be real, the less real it inevitably becomes because doubts multiply under analysis. Watt searches for absolute, irrefutable proof about the pot that he observes in the house, about the reality of the Galls, father and son, who come to tune a piano, quite uselessly because the mice have eaten most of the felts and hammer heads and the strings are in flitters. He wonders about the meaning and purpose of his own activities and those of others, but the more he investigates the less sure he is of anything. *Watt* is certainly not about God looking for man, which could be one interpretation of the second half of *Molloy*. If, as it appears, it is about man looking for God, then he is as unsuccessful as the rest of us who do not subscribe to a fundamentalist faith. Beckett ultimately demonstrates that all attempts to prove reality by perception, definition and thought, are a form of intellectual masturbation. The only external reality that matters is the misery of the human condition. Literature cannot improve it, nor in any significant way can social engineering. The answer is not to be born at all. If one is born, one waits to die. The only real answer to life is laughter and meditation, but the first is in essence bitter protest or despair, the second a self indulgence without purpose. Philosophy passes the time, like mathematics, and can be interesting, but it will always consist of increasing the number of questions, not in finding final answers.

Mr Knott does however want to be recognised, that is to say, he wants his presence, if not seen, to be at least known. There is no Beckettian dualism more important in his work than the paradoxical desire and need to disappear, to escape from the world and its preoccupation's and to be nothing (Geulincx) and, conversely, to be recognised, remembered, and to have lived for a purpose. Beckett has identified one major twentieth-century human anguish, which arises partly from the loss of religion, with its promises of an after-life as a sort of continuum and reward, partly out of the great movement of peoples and individuals which has separated millions from their roots, so that it is seldom possible for such people to feel any more that they are a part of a continuing family stretching back into the historical past and forward into the future, and partly, perhaps the most important factor of all, because of the growth of individual consciousness, through education and democracy, so that the developing person sees himself, not as part of a race or tribe where the group and not the individual is important, as with bees and ants, and where the individual is expected to sacrifice himself willingly for the good of the group, but as a person of importance, and value in his own right. The thought of being born, of going through all the anxieties and sufferings of life, with perhaps a few tolerable years for those lucky enough to be born into a culture that allows such a benefit, then to die, to disappear, and soon to be completely forgotten, all traces of life obliterated: that is a thought that cannot be entertained, but of course it is. In one work after another Beckett tries to bring up the theme of recognition. Everyone has to know that in some way he or she matters, that the life lived has had some point. The need to be recognised and remembered becomes the motivation behind the creation of new concepts about human life and destiny, surfacing many times in Beckett's work.

In *Watt*, it is Mr Knott who wants his existence to be realised, and if he is meant to represent God, then his need is rather different from the human one for recognition. Christians go to worship, to praise God and to pray to him. Why an omnipotent being who has created everything and by definition should be self-sufficient, needs to be worshipped is a mystery, and can only be explained politically. In ages of absolutist rule by kings, princes or emperors, it is essential that God should be represented as being as much as possible like those absolute rulers on earth, who thereby take their authority from him. Kings are certainly willing to be worshipped, especially if we go back a century or two. And on a family level, the father is the creator of his children, and he is certainly willing to be at least admired by his children, while mothers take on a more protective form of authority, idealised in Catholicism as the Madonna. Should God not be above all that? Praise is simply an active form of worship, for which the same royal or family analogy holds true. As for prayer, it is a form of begging, familiar to every father, and of course to every monarch. It is, then, obvious that the God of the monotheistic religions is always based on authoritarian human models. In a later chapter I shall return to Beckett's view of God, whose need of recognition, where he or his counterpoint is portrayed in the writings, would seem to have little importance other than the realisation that man always sees God in his own likeness, only bigger.

The human need for recognition is something altogether different. It is or has become a basic human need, and Beckett the creative writer has looked for a new mythology to satisfy it. In *Waiting for Godot* we are led through a conventional theatrical build-up towards a climax, Vladimir's great speech near the end of the play which appears to be modelled on the 'To be or not to be' soliloquy in *Hamlet*. It makes the same kind of impact on an audience and would seems to sum up Beckett's philosophy of despair, reprieved, but only just, at the last moment, by the speaker grasping the rescue line and returning to the present with 'What have I said?'

Only when Beckett directed his own play for the first time, at the Schiller Theatre in Berlin, did a quite different climax emerge. It was the appearance of the boy at the end, a different boy, according to his story, from the brother who had come at the end of the first act to tell the two tramps that Godot would not come that day, but would surely come tomorrow. It is not the bad news he brings that so upsets Vladimir, but the boy's air of never having seen him before. He wants to be remembered, however marginally, by a boy who will outlive him by many years; he must impress on the boy a memory that someone like him once existed. Vladimir's pointless and unnecessary violence has only this one purpose, to be remembered. Another boy, similar in description, appears at the end of the television play, *Ghost Trio*. He represents the future, as all boys do in Beckett, and once again he is probably there to remember the protagonist. There is however another explanation as well, that he is the man's own younger self, the future to be that was, remembered by the protagonist as the embodiment of all his young hopes.[25]

The mythology that Beckett invents to replace the standard expectation of a heaven or hell waiting for us is very simple, and owes something to spiritualism and to Buddhism. It is that the voices of the dead are all around us, that they are as unaware of us as we of them, and that they talk 'each to himself' endlessly. The conceit occurs first in *Waiting for Godot*, although there is something like it in his early story *Assumption* (1929) where a dead man leaves his body and walks around his old familiar surroundings. We get three such 'dead voices' in *Play*, where Beckett has put their heads on the top of man-sized jars and they are moved to speak by an inquisitorial light that flashes from one head to another. They speak in jerks, going back over their lives, telling the story of a three-sided relationship between the man, his wife and his mistress, lives which came to some unhappy, but unspecified, end. The story, related in turn by the three, each talking to himself or herself as the light flashes from face to face, is given to the audience twice, in not quite the same sequence, and the second time round both the voices and the light decline in power. This could be part of a Buddhist concept, the three dead beings waiting to be returned to life in a reincarnation or it could be simply a Dantesque punishment, taking place in an after-life to confront past sins. Certainly the idea developed out of *Waiting for Godot*, and there may even be some slight influence from Sartre's *Huis Clos*, where three dead people in the hell of an enclosed room, each two not being able to stand the presence of the other, all see the truths of their past conduct gradually emerge, and where—a telling detail—they get a glimpse of the world they have left every time they are thought of or talked about with such glimpses becoming rarer as time passes. There are often many, not necessarily contradictory, interpretations of Beckett's concepts. In the case of *Play*, the fading of voices and light may be simply the fading of consciousness in the brain when the body is already dead. Beckett was much fascinated by severed heads; during the Fifties there was a macabre experiment in Paris where two guillotined heads of executed criminals managed to respond to questions by raising and lowering their eyelids some time after the heads had been amputated. Beckett could not have been unaware of this widely reported event which became part of his collection of useful images. The fading of consciousness while the mind tries desperately to stay alive is present in his novels from *Malone Dies* to *How It Is*. If the voices are ghosts, then we also have ghosts in *Ghost Trio*, *Not I*, and *Footfalls* and probably in *Ohio Impromptu* as well.

In *Not I* the voice is a woman who is being interrogated by a silent, robed figure who does nothing except make a gesture of resignation or despair each time the woman's voice, babbling on with its memories about another who is obviously herself, breaks off to interject a 'Not I', disclaiming her own role. The auditor was removed for the television version. She too is one of the 'dead voices'. *Footfalls* is more of a pure ghost story that any other Beckett work in that the only real character is the mother whose voice we hear in the first scene while her imaginary, aborted daughter paces up and down on the floor below, visible to the audience, which the mother is not. The daughter, who was never properly born, is a ghost, a fragment of the imagination of the mother whose purpose is to remember her when she is dead, but in a further Beckett *coup de théâtre*, the daughter invents another ghost who will be dimly glimpsed in a dark church by those who will be alive in the future. So the ghost that remembers the mother will herself be remembered, or at least seen. Metaphorically that is how we are remembered in reality. Our memories, and the indirect knowledge of past ancestors, gets dimmer with time. Everything finally is forgotten. The play catches the essence of our delusions, and perhaps also explains the reason why we so fascinated by the idea of ghosts, even when we have no religious belief. They represent survival.

Although the need to be recognised comes through most forcefully in *Waiting for Godot* and subsequent works, the theme is there earlier. Descartes' *Cogito Ergo Sum* has its roots in a need to exist even if only for oneself and all attempts to prove one's existence must stem from that need. *Watt* is Beckett's most perverse and puzzling novel because it is so diverse, the outer sections enfolding the central two, which describe Watt's attempts to prove the existence of everything he sees or does not see, but imagines. Cartesian logic is carried to extremes, every possible combination of proof and possibility, or probability or improbability, being explored, always with another new special case, coming suddenly to mind. The author interjects himself into the second section, in the first person, telling the reader that everything he knows comes from Watt, who has told him of his observations and deliberations. The inconsequence of many of the things that Watt tries to prove does not in any way deflect him from his logic. As everything is told to the author by Watt, or rather everything is being told to Watt by the narrator invented by the author, who thereby becomes a character in the novel, an extra element of suspicion is thereby introduced. We later learn that this character is called Sam, and that he is a lunatic, so the whole structure of logic, of truth and falsehood, reality and unreality, becomes doubly suspect.

We can never be quite sure of what we are told by someone who is talking from personal experience, because he might not be telling the truth, or he might be telling what he believes to be the truth, which is not the truth, or his logic may be wrong. The difficulty becomes greater when we are hearing something at second hand, such as the narrator telling us of what he had heard from Watt. The farther the information is from the original source the less can we rely on it. This applies to all history, written or oral, and it certainly applies to the Bible. Beckett's suspicion of second-hand knowledge and logic is evident in *Watt*, and the theme of suspicion crops up later in his work, notably in *What Where*, where an inquisitor is sent out to investigate and extract (by torture) a confession from a third party and then has to undergo the same ordeal himself because it is not believed that he did not extract the confession. The origins of *What Where* may also lie in Beckett's wartime experiences and the ordeals of his friends who were captured. All attitudes are investigated in *Watt* and there is no conclusion other than there can be no absolute proof because of the fallibility of the mind and the unwillingness of an agnostic tendency to believe anything. The dichotomy between philosophy, which is the thirst for knowledge, and everyday life, where logical proof of what one knows through one's senses is of little general interest to others, is well illustrated. Beckett goes off on several tangents from the central subject matter, which is Watt's need to prove everything, all the time, however unimportant, in order to give us discursive pictures of people and their attitudes of only marginal relevance to Watt's quest. It is a picaresque novel, enjoyable but messy and very fragmented; it is probably fair to take Beckett's little footnote to the Addenda of the book seriously: 'Only fatigue and disgust prevented its incorporation': the 'its' in this case is a collection of aphorisms, phrases, partial or complete sentences and paragraphs, even whole poems, put together at the end of the novel as notes, originally intended to be used by the author at some point but never incorporated. It is the novelist mocking himself. Beckett's Commonplace Book, which he gave to the archive at Reading University, is full of such jottings. We must also remember the circumstances of *Watt*'s first publication. Written during the war, it was in 1945 probably only a motley collection of episodes and pages that he later put into order in Paris. Richard Seaver, then a member of the *Merlin* group, had heard about this novel written in English from Jérôme Lindon, Beckett's first French publisher, who could not read English, and asked him if he could see the manuscript. Beckett dropped in on a *Merlin* editorial meeting one evening and silently handed it over in a brown paper parcel. It became one of the first 'literary works' to appear from *Olympia Press*, but their editorial standards left much to be desired, so the cleaning-up, filling in of gaps and other anomalies never took place. When the *Watt* manuscript was given to *Merlin*, *Waiting for Godot* had already been written, the *Trilogy* had been published, and Beckett almost certainly had lost interest in his old, pre-1945 work. Much of it must have been wearying to write, and it would have been surprising if he had found the time and the inclination to fill in the discrepancies and tidy it up in his then frame of mind. It is the most unfinished of his novels, but also one of the funniest and, and in its discursions, the most theatrical. Read aloud, it is a delight.

Watt was published in 1953. No other Beckett work is so eccentric, or so difficult to describe. It starts as a comic erotic novel, follows Watt in his perambulations on his way to Mr Knott's house in a fairly conventional style and then gives us Arsene's long and rambling monologue, a rant at the human condition. Then come the two central sections, full of combinations of movements, routines, quests and investigations. The first is a mockery of Cartesian philosophy, not inappropriate for a writer who had just spent three years hiding from the Germans in a little hill village where the contrast between the intellectual life of prewar Dublin and Paris and those of his circumstances at the time could not have been more different. Mirthless humour is most appropriate here, and there is much of it. But it is also a spoof of scholasticism, and a very good one, asking questions that can never be answered, and that in any case are pointless. But even when mocked, philosophy is still philosophy and always a search for meaning. Watt's quest, like Murphy's, is doomed to frustration, but for the reader willing to follow all his labyrinthine combinations of logical reasoning there is much humour, interesting stylistic originality and perhaps a lesson in logic.

Section II of *Watt* would appear to be about man's quest for God. It ends with the arrival of Arthur to replace Watt as Watt replaced Arsene, and Watt then moves from Mr Knott's house to another building. In section III there is a change of tone and Sam is now relating his relationship with Watt in the first person. Watt is lodged in another pavilion, his garden adjacent to Sam's and their friendship is very odd. They walk and talk, they kill the birds and crush the birds' eggs, all in a very natural way, and in one of the most controversial episodes they make friends with the rats, feeding them out of their hands 'now a nice fat frog, or a baby thrush. Or seizing suddenly a plump young rat . . . we would feed it to its mother, or its father, or its brother, or its sister, or to some less fortunate relative.'[26] Is this a parody of the earth, where we are fed by God, where everything eats everything, where pity is unknown to nature? The next sentence is revealing: 'It was on these occasions, we agreed, after an exchange of views, that we came nearest to God.'[27]

Beckett we know was interested in Manicheism, which blends Christianity with the Eastern meditative philosophies and religions. To the Cathars, it was the devil who invented the world and the world is therefore in essence evil; man, always at a disadvantage, has to conquer the nature in himself, his desires, impulses and attraction towards emotion, the spring of cruelty, hatred, greed and other unattractive human impulses, as well as of love. He can only counter the dark side of the world by self-sacrifice and abnegation, by denying the flesh and the will. Coming at the problem from a different perspective, Schopenhauer was basically saying the same thing. Although Descartes's followers who preached poverty, Geulincx and Malebranche, stayed within Christian orthodoxy, the manicheist tendency is apparent in their work. When Sam (although we must not confuse the character who is narrating with the author who invented the narrator, we can, I think, assume that the presence of the name is deliberate and may be intended to portray the dark or philosophically uncontrolled side of Beckett's character) speaks of his nearness to God in what is deliberately meant to disgust or upset the reader, he is making it clear that his God is not the 'gentle Jesus' of a child's prayer, nor the God of love and justice.

It is clear from any close reading of Beckett's work that the writer himself, preoccupied by the search for meaning in the world, unable to come to any conclusion about purpose, unable to believe in any creed or even any personal philosophy other than maintaining a dogged stoicism, finds in the end a kind of comfort from an acceptance of darkness and pain. That is the situation of most of his later protagonists, imprisoned in the dark, usually, although not always, in some physical pain, but always the victim of a restlessly probing mind, boring holes into the appearances of reality and unreality, as if to find something or nothing behind them, as he puts it in his letter to Axel Kaun. He said to me once: 'All I ever wanted to do was put my forehead against the cliff-rock and move it a fraction of a millimetre.' The presence of evil cannot be denied: the most casual look around reveals it everywhere, it is always in a dominating position, and all that can be done by those endowed with moral instincts is to combat it, under duress, with every possible sacrifice and personal inconvenience. Perhaps the first step is to recognise the evil in oneself, the original sin (not only of the curse of Adam in our mythology, but the inadvertent sin of being born). That is what Vladimir and Estragon are doing, although they still do not understand the whole situation as well as their creator does. Many of Beckett's characters, Molloy, for instance, are victims, but they are anything but 'good' or 'moral'. Molloy's greatest satisfaction is to wreak havoc on the body of someone weaker than himself; one punishes others in revenge for the punishment one has oneself received.

In *Watt* Beckett clearly indicates that if God has influence in the world, it must be an evil influence. God is therefore either the Devil or so remote from the world of man that he lets the Devil do what he wants. That still leaves us with the problem of purpose: is there any purpose at all? Is it conceivable that the whole of existence, about which we are constantly learning more by probing the infinitely large 'outer space', and the infinitely small, (the inside of the atom) and the chemical structure of our existence, has no meaning? Could everything we know and perceive just be an accident, a mistake that has taken on form and continuity? These thoughts are always present, becoming a transmutation of both concept and language, as the author moves into his late work, particularly *Worstward Ho*, which is to the Beckett canon what *The Tempest* is to Shakespeare's.

In his early poem *The Vulture*, influenced by Goethe's *Harzreise in Winter*, Beckett gave a picture of a vulture soaring over the earth, the whole external world being inside, not outside, the brain, existing there until the brain itself is offal. This is not only a poetic but also a Lockian concept, one that is also in accord with the theories of Bishop Berkeley. In the Goethe poem man is driven by his predestination to success or failure, and this vision of man as prey is one that Beckett may have remembered later when writing *Molloy*. But it is the progress of the mind towards decay that attracted Beckett to *Harzreise in Winter*. The empty brain must of course be hollow, like a skull, and in his later work Beckett develops the concept in a way that is both poetic and metaphysical, with spectral figures inside that cavity, moving through the eternity of space and time. The meaning, other than as a poetic image, can only be the subject of much speculation, but its genesis is clear: the philosophers Beckett had absorbed at Trinity had already used imagination as an outward-bound image to delimit and limit the growth of knowledge and understanding. Take Hume for instance:

> Let us fix our attention out of ourselves as much as possible; let us chace (sic) our imagination to the heavens, or to the utmost limits of the universe; we never really advance a step beyond ourselves, nor can we conceive any kind of existence, but those perceptions, which have appear'd in that narrow compass. This is the universe of the imagination, nor have we any idea of what is there produc'd.[28]

There is always a great deal behind Beckett's metaphors: none is more striking than the image he gives in his short text *Imagination Dead Imagine*, where two huddled figures are enclosed inside a skull-like capsule hurtling through space. They are not quite dead, but not quite alive either, possessing sensations and awareness, but frozen in their confinement.

Like Murphy's mind in its three phases, the figures see their environment change from light to darkness, they suffer pain, they sweat and freeze: could it be that they are awaiting reincarnation, to go through the life cycle once again? Could this also be the fate of the 'dead voices' reliving their pasts until their karma releases them into a new existence? Beckett's metaphysics may be purely in the world of speculative imagination, but in spite of the author's basic disbelief in all religious dogma, one often feels that he is driven by his own genius to create a world of philosophical possible existence that might be or eventually become believable to others, just as Dante's fictional metaphysics became part of a Catholic mythology that was almost treated as a dogma.

Certainly the thought of returning to life was one of Beckett's great fears. The intellectual superiority of Buddhism over monotheistic religion, and the logic of reincarnation with the concept of eventual ethical justice was not lost on him. Although Beckett constantly stated his lack of any religious belief, he never called himself an atheist, and no one can accuse him of total nihilism, although attempts to link him to the existentialism of Sartre and the negativism of Heidegger are interesting. There is always a dualism in Beckett; the 'perhaps' is the breaking point of the tension between his opposites, hope and despair, the material and the immaterial, the something and the nothing. If reincarnation is a fear, he rubs it in like salt in a wound.

Although a stoic, always intellectually in the presence of death, both longing for oblivion and dreading the form it might take in the great uncertainty of all things, Beckett was never unaware that his own created world of suffering continuing after death might well be his own fate. The questing of Watt was really a mockery of his own personal search for meaning, founded on the models he knew but it becomes constantly bogged down in language (which at different times he regarded as both his friend and his enemy, as he makes clear in many, often contradictory, pronouncements), in the novel's calculations of all the possible courses of action or of inaction, its permutations of the trivial and of the slightly less trivial, for how else could a questor such as Watt determine where meaning lay and what was important? In any case trivia is what life is mostly about for the average person. *In Act Without Words* 2 Beckett reduces the human day to waking up, dressing to prepare for it, and undressing and going to sleep at the end of it. His two contrasting protagonists, one the positive, successful character, the other the negative failure, live the same life and share the same suit of clothes: their opposite attitudes to life cannot change their equal destiny.

Beckett's image of a capsule hurtling through space, which he makes us see as a skull-like cavity from which the mind itself appears itself to be missing, [except in so far as (in *Imagination Dead Imagine*) there are crouched figures within the cavity who appear to have minds of a sort], has many variations in his work. The ability of the mind to leave the body and travel outside it, and to return, is believed by some spiritualist groups and by many Buddhist, and appears frequently in fiction. It is a concept that could only intrigue Beckett as very desirable; it is of course, like everything else outside everyday possibilities, perfectly possible through dreams. Mind travel appears to happen in *Stirrings Still*. In *Worstward Ho*, where we get a picture of human development from the creation of man up to his moving adventurously but unhappily out into the cosmos, there is a quite startling vision of the immensity of space to be conquered, a pinhole admitting the dimmest possible amount of light into what is left of skull in the great circling void. It appears to owe something to Ptolemy and the medieval image of heaven (the stars being pinholes in the firmament admitting heavenly light to our eyes at night):

> No move and sudden all far. All least. Three pins. One pinhole.
> In dimmest dim. Vasts apart. At bounds of boundless void.
> Whence no farther.[29]

Beckett never denies the reality of human progress or that man can acquire even greater knowledge and understanding of the universe in which we are individually and collectively a tiny, insignificant mote, and as an investigative thinker he

is fascinated by the idea of it. But he always asks, by implication, if all the progress is worth all the inevitable suffering
that is the human lot, and the anguish of our consciousness
in the face of its own necessary extinction. His answer is a
resounding No, and that was before the arrival of new horrors
in the world during the Nineties, which he never lived to see.
It is not enough for an aware consciousness that has learned
to value its own existence to be simply a link in a chain, even
if one's personal contribution to the chain's future growth is
likely to be remembered, although the prospect of future fame
is always a spur to a creative mind. Beckett was not immune
to that spur, although he wanted to be. He got round this
difficulty in saying that the artist has an 'obligation to
express', outside his will, that he cannot avoid. It is akin to
the final temptation (the sin of pride) of the martyr, as dramatised in T. S. Eliot's *Murder in the Cathedral*.

The 'obligation to express' (to be creative) of *The Duthuit
Dialogues* is certainly fuelled by the need to be remembered.
Discussing with an Irish friend why Beckett decided to be
buried in a graveyard rather than be cremated, I suddenly
realised that it was, of course, part of that same need. Many
Beckett pilgrims visit the simple granite slab in Montparnasse
cemetery under which his remains lie. Yet he must have been
torn. He admired the Marquis de Sade's desire to be buried
in a forest, the spot unmarked, and to disappear totally from
human memory. But Beckett's final poems, reflecting his state
of mind as he approached death, with all their stoical acceptance of the end of thought and anguish, and the peace of
oblivion, in no way resemble Sade's stated desire to be forgotten. The tomb, easily found in the cemetery, is the proof.

Murphy is imprisoned in his mind which is imprisoned in
his body. Watt is imprisoned in his need to understand what
cannot be understood and not believed by someone who is
unable to accept second-hand evidence, not even the evidence
of his own senses; nor does he have the ability to identify a
nomenclature with the object known through its name, such
as a pot. With the great postwar *Trilogy* Beckett moved to
another world, away from the metaphorical embodiments of

philosophy in eccentric human form, to a grimmer and more recognisable setting, one nearer parable than metaphor, where philosophical concepts are still examined, but the writing is much more direct. In so far as his gift for the comic is still present, it is more redolent of the mirthless, the dianoetic laugh, than the bitter or the hollow laugh, though they too are present. In the earlier Beckett novels, all the characters belong and live in the same world, even if they do not understand each other. Murphy is seen by Mr Kelly, Celia's father, rather the way Beckett's parents saw him, as a work-shy wastrel in spite of his academic brilliance, but still belonging to the same world. Molloy on the other hand sees himself as very different from the rest of humanity, not part of 'their world'.[30] He is the wild quarry, the animal hunted for sport, trying to be obsequious where he cannot be invisible, 'more toad than rat'. Only the second part of *Molloy*, Moran's story, harks back to the picaresque style of *Murphy*, *Watt* and *Mercier and Camier*, and Moran belongs to a conventional world that has no place for Molloy. The picture of a mind disintegrating into panic, of thought running amok, and the skull emptying itself to 'offal', and ultimately to the emptiness of a hollow cavity, the dominant image of Beckett's fictions from the late Forties onward, starts in *Malone Dies*. It finds its most terrifying expression in *The Unnamable*, which is followed, some years later, by *How It Is*, with its very similar ending. After that we are in the world of the late short fictions, some of them really highly-condensed novels, usually giving a single, startlingly original image of the human predicament in metaphors where the human anguish is implicit rather that stated.

The *Trilogy* and what follows cannot be described as a set of philosophical novels like the earlier ones. What emerges from them is not the illustration of philosophical concepts, but rather a presentation of the world from which philosophical and moral conclusions can be drawn. They are an indictment of the whole creation of the world in which we live, whether that world is the product of some uncaring first cause or of a monotheistic authoritarian God or even of pure accident. Beckett forces us to face what every social, political and commercial institution is programmed to stop us facing: the whole horror of the human predicament, not knowing where we come from, why we are here and where we are going. It explains why the greatest literary genius of his century, while recognised, is so little read and so deliberately misunderstood.

3

Man's Inhumanity and the Search for Love

Beckett was a contemplative writer who lived during one of the world's periods of greatest brutality. As a young man he was torn between his background, the upper-middle class world of professional and comfortably situated families in which he grew up, and the world of intellectual bohemia to which he was attracted and where he knew he belonged. Beckett's circumstances in youth were more stable financially than those of Joyce—at least until he left home—and it was in any case less easy for a Protestant to become a bohemian intellectual than for a middle-class Catholic. By bohemian I mean an attitude, a willingness to be part of a non-competitive community, free-living, sharing, art-minded, not concerned with appearances—exactly the opposite of what we understand by the 'Protestant ethic.' Beckett's literature stems from and is powered by the conflict between his family and early educational background on the one hand, and his own inclination on the other. Although he became a bohemian intellectual *par excellence*, he never lost the world he had left, carrying it within him like a growth that both fed and poisoned him. Beckett's many dualisms began with the opposition between his background and character.

As a young man he could not help noticing the difference between the lives and living conditions of the Irish poor, overwhelmingly Catholic, and the rich and comfortably off, overwhelmingly Protestant. The independence of Eire had not immediately changed the class or religious relations of the country: property was still mainly owned by the Anglo-Irish Protestant ascendancy. When he went to France in 1930 Beckett naturally fell in with the academic left-bank intellectual community, to which he had access as a result of the annual exchange of talented student lecturers between Trinity and the Sorbonne; he also fell in with the artistic Irish crowd in Paris of which James Joyce was the leading light. Their values became his; free-living, improvident, and intellectually exciting. Talent, ideas and conversation were what mattered and *carpe diem*.

During the next few years he visited Germany, saw at first hand the bully-boy tactics of the Nazis, and, once they were in power the resulting destruction of intellectual freedom, with even more menacing dangers for Jews and dissidents. Being by his own choice in France throughout the whole German Occupation, he learned, not only that the top strata of society can be indifferent to the misery of the masses, which he already knew, but how severe can be the ruthlessness of the conqueror towards the conquered. The use of torture to punish or to extract information, and for its own sake to give pleasure to the sadistic, became common practice. In his first-hand observation and understanding of how humans behaved under such conditions he saw among the oppressed how some behaved shamefully for personal gain, or in a cowardly fashion out of fear, whereas others, a small but significant minority, behaved with magnificent courage, knowing that their actions could well bring disaster on themselves and their communities. Beckett discovered the spring from which his writing and pursuit of meaning could flow.

The great works of Beckett's middle period, written with a sword of Damocles hanging over his head—he believed that a tumour growing in his cheek would allow him little time to live[31]—brought out the contrasts that he had observed in human behaviour. Although the stress of the German Occupation dramatised these contrasts, the basic facts of human nature are always the same. Any idealistic view Beckett might have had before the war of human perfectibility, vanished during it. The comic eccentricities of ordinary people—and it was his observation of Dublin people that he had best described in his early novels—no longer lighten his work to make the reader chuckle. His humour moved towards the mirthless, the laugh at unhappiness. Molloy, one of his most extraordinary creations, is too earthy to be eccentric. He is basically an observer, one to whom things are done, rather than a doer, but he has his moments of action when the opportunity is there, as when he assaults the charcoal burner, a man more decrepit than himself. One gives pain in revenge for the pain one has received.

There is nothing in Beckett's depiction of Molloy to make us like him, but we understand and empathise because all of us see part of ourselves in this prototypal human being whom everyone despises but who is still capable of attracting members of the opposite sex, if only because most women will take up with any man rather than none. His story is told in the first person, which at the time was an innovation for Beckett. Molloy does not see himself as belonging to the human race proper and refers to 'their planet'. He is a natural target for the police, and the object of unwanted charity from the social worker who offers him a cup of tea:

> Let me tell you this, when social workers offer you free, gratis and for nothing, something to hinder you from swooning, which with them is an obsession, it is useless to recoil, they will pursue you to the ends of the earth, the vomitory in their hands. . .Against the charitable gesture there is no defence that I know of. . .To him who is nothing, it is forbidden not to relish filth.[32]

And in one of the most vivid episodes we see Molloy as a hunted animal, like a fox or stag whose pursuit is preceded by the hunt breakfast, the stirrup cup, the assembling of hounds and the blowing of horns. He creeps close to the walls to escape notice

> bowed down like a good boy, oozing with obsequiousness, having nothing to hide, hiding from mere terror, looking neither right nor left, hiding but not provocatively, ready to come out, to smile, to listen, to crawl, nauseating but not pestilent, less rat then toad.[33]

This was very much the situation of Beckett when, as a fugitive from the Nazis, he avoided capture in the Paris streets and eventually bicycled down to the south, ending up in Roussillon, where he hid until the liberation. There he found his real-life partner in exile, Henri Hayden, a Dutch Jewish painter, and this pairing became the model for some of the couples that would later appear in his writings, like Mercier and Camier, but especially Vladimir and Estragon.

What emerges from Beckett's studies of human nature, in the theatre and in his novels, shows signs of Augustinian pre-destination: man is what he is, each one different, each in his private hell, living a life trapped in a situation that he did not and could not choose, as good or as bad as his individual nature allows him to be: he is unimprovable and unchange-able in any significant way, trapped as the protagonists of Greek drama were trapped by the Gods, but in our own case by the lottery of a malign nature or, in Calvinist theology, by God's decision before our birth. Modern science seems to confirm this: we are all the product of our DNA, which decides what we are and how we behave. If we are all born with original sin, it must be part of our human nature and therefore cannot be evaded. But as we have seen, Beckett believed that the original sin lay in being born at all; birth is foisted on us by our parents. And life is the punishment for it.

Beckett is really restating what the Greek playwrights said in another way, that the only antidote to this continuance of human suffering must lie in an awareness of consequence, so those responsible enough to realise what the consequences are likely to be, can develop the discipline to overcome nature's compulsion to procreate. Nature has of course already under-mined that sense of responsibility by giving us emotions that make us fall in love and sexual desires of which generation is the likely result. Nature has also endowed woman more than man with the desire to reproduce, a desire so strong that it overcomes the necessary pain and unpleasantness of child-birth. For this reason Beckett casts woman in a highly stylised, even biblical, role: she is the temptress, the whore, the destroyer of peace and of intellectual activity, forcing her physical demands upon man, who becomes torn between his natural lust and his desire for freedom. Beckett's women are strong women, powerful in their ability to overcome man's attempts to avoid domesticity, and to put aside the unwanted realities that face them daily, whether it is their own aging (*Happy Days*), the inconvenience of outside events or the man's reluctance to become their passive slave and provider. The female praying mantises that eat their mates, even during the act of copulation, are, symbolically, not far from that human situation, especially where the male artist is concerned. To the genuine artist nothing must ever be more important than his art. This should apply to the female artist as well, but there is more likely to be conflict in her case, the resolution of which, for some at least, would seem to lie in pairing with another artist.

The analogy of the praying mantis seems to be quite clear in Beckett's work. The male submits, questioning all the time, because his gonads force him into mating, but what the artist really needs is only occasional relief from the necessary loneliness of his creative situation.

> Love brings out the worst in man and no error. But what kind of love was this, exactly? Love-passion? Somehow I think not. That's the priapic one, is it not? Or is this a different variety? There are so many, are there not? All equally more delicious, are they not? Platonic love, for example, there's another just occurs to me. Its disinterested.[34]

The male praying mantis dies so that the female can reproduce the species and in essence the human female demands much the same sacrifice. Man submits then wants to escape. The growth of a socially mobile technological society has given him this ability, although normally he simply escapes with someone else, and his problems begin all over again. Homosexuality is a different escape, allowing for love without procreative consequence in new life, and it is strange that homosexual thinkers have not yet taken up Beckett as a guru, offering an additional moral justification for their culture. Beckett himself much attracted women, was attracted by them, but resisted any procreative urge on ethical grounds. It is the dilemma of the artist, poignantly dramatised in *Krapp's Last Tape* to choose between sexual and connubial bliss (for as long as it lasts), and the freedom to devote oneself entirely to one's art. A domesticated Beckett could never have become the supreme artist he was.

Beckett had many homosexuals among his friends, and his

obvious approval of a life style in which children had no part is observable in all his work: homosexuals tend to be kinder and more caring with each other than heterosexuals, where there is always a trace of sex war in a relationship. Beckett's male couples are in a sense sexless: their relationships depend on affection, mutual need, loneliness mitigated and the ability to share. Women play no immediate part in their lives, although they may have in the past. Interestingly, in *Waiting for Godot* although Vladimir and Estragon discuss a great many things, they do not discuss women. It is through the sexual memories of his characters, especially in *Molloy*, that Beckett gives us his views on sex, not through discussion. And these views are cruelly funny and extremely jaundiced. In *First Love* he provides his most powerful and naturalistic account of a heterosexual relationship, in which the man submits to sex, with many acute observations on the nature of the sexual woman, who is here, as always in Beckett, the aggressor; when the inevitable consequences arrive, the man flees, not without guilt, but out of his personal necessity, in panic.

Sex is always portrayed in Beckett with a mixture of fascination and disgust. He had all the normal instincts and understood them in biological terms, but distrusted them as Adam distrusted the temptations of Eve. His disgust, well described in his fictions, of the whole process of generation is rooted in a philosophical conviction: bringing life into an evil world must be evil, therefore the circumstances of birth with all their mess of blood and water and pain become not only unpleasant, but part of that evil. Beckett's father, described in *Company*, with understanding and affection, but in this instance as if the author were in his place, goes off for an all-day tramp in the mountains so as not to be present at Sam's birth on a Good Friday. He is disappointed on his return to find at the backdoor at nightfall that 'Labour was still in swing'. He retreats to his car in the garage until he is told it is 'Over at last'. Beckett, with great feeling, repeats the last word: 'Over!'[35] A new long misery has begun, his own.

If Beckett could have separated fornication from its consequences in his mind, difficult given his upbringing, he might have been able to view sex very differently—and of course in practical terms he did, because we live in a world of widespread contraception—but the difficulty lies in the nature of women. Infertile women, who Beckett would have considered blessed in providence, still go to extraordinary lengths to conceive, totally ignoring the urgent need of an overpopulated world to bring down its birth rate. In *Molloy*, where we get detailed descriptions of the sexual act, the dominant reaction is disgust. Love is not denigrated as such, but because it leads to sex, which leads to new life and, consequently, future suffering.

The moment of generation, as John Pilling points out,[36] 'is where eternity enters time, and being enters existence'. It is the beginning of death when, as Schopenhauer puts it, we return to where we came from, and Beckett, although having Molloy describe his months in the womb as 'the only endurable, just endurable, period of my enormous history',[37] a period of limbo, tends in his writing not to separate the moment of generation and the moment of birth, and he also sees birth and death as almost simultaneous events: 'the same moment, the same instant', or as he beautifully puts it in a poem previously quoted, 'to live the space of a door / that opens and shuts'. The identification of birth and death comes up many times in Beckett's work, most famously in Pozzo's departing speech:

> Astride of the grave and a difficult birth. Down in the hole, lingeringly, the grave-digger puts on the forceps.[38]

Interestingly, in his early short book on *Proust* (1931), he almost says the opposite in a striking figure: 'by no expedient of macabre transubstantiation can the grave-sheets serve as swaddling-clothes.'[39] This was in a different context which will be considered in the next chapter, but the image is very similar to that of the grave-digger and probably inspired it.

Our short lives are, after all, the tiniest of instants in the progress of time and eternity, less than the natural lives of many other animals, fish, crustaceans and reptiles, not to speak of trees. The smallness of man's life in eternity and of man himself in space, is a theme to which Beckett frequently returns. It is infinitely better not to be born, and inevitably if one is to reject the creation of new life, one should also, for safety, reject love, because woman's instinct will always be to produce. Shaw's superman is what woman is striving to produce, a man becoming the God he has invented in his own image. But that will simply be a more evolved form of man, his suffering increasing with his intelligence and knowledge. Compared to primitive man, we already are *Superman*, but no happier for it.

Beckett in his own life accepted the love of women, always with a certain reluctance, but he insured that there was no outcome in new life. He was attracted to women who were intelligent, buxom, *boulotte*, cheerful, outspoken and outgoing. They all had an aggressive or dominating streak, the opposite of his own nature. Beckett in his relationships with women tended to be passive, as much out of shyness as for any other reason. *First Love* is close enough, in its comic way, to his own experience; its comic elements are however horrific, as is the ending. Beckett's own sexual needs always conflicted with his intellectual asceticism. In his awareness of the love of others it was not too hard to detect, not in any personal way— Beckett was too gentle and courteous for that—a certain sadness at seeing nature once again triumphant and continuing the progress of human suffering. Mature love, past the childbearing age, was another matter, and caused him no *arrière pensée*. Homosexual relationships fell into the same category. The artistic world is not judgemental about homosexuality, but it does notice it and comment. Beckett did not. Companionship and friendship among males is what he depicts in his most moving works: it is the antidote to loneliness, to facing the terrors of the everyday world and those others present in one's own mind, and without the complications of sex. Companionship helps to make life tolerable; it is the sharing of misery, an important part of the Beckett ethic.

The addition of sex in homosexual relationships is of no importance, except in that it may enhance them to the point of creating a form of happiness, about which Beckett always had minor mixed feelings, emotional more than intellectual. I have nothing against happiness, he frequently said, I just don't happen to have a talent for it. It was as alien to his nature as a flower garden to a fish. And yet he could himself, at times, evidence a semblance of happiness for brief periods. These were times when he was able to forget himself, engaging in or watching sport, or playing chess, or talking and drinking with friends, or playing the piano, perhaps most of all when working with actors in the theatre, providing they were actors on his own wavelength. It was the comradeship of working together, in rehearsal, especially after he had formed a bond with actors who respected him and trusted his way of getting the effects he wanted, in which he found relief from the long solitary hours at his desk, sometimes in Paris, but more frequently at Ussy in the quiet of the Marne countryside. On his own he wrote and endlessly revised and reworked his fictions and play texts; lonely work. Beckett was never forthcoming about his working methods, and would talk, if at all, of spending hours looking out of the window, doing nothing. But his manuscripts tell a different story, of the meticulous weighing of words, the cuts and additions, the rewriting and revision, the frequent switches from French to English or vice-versa. But this was work, not enjoyment. Rehearsing was work too, but—if he felt well and if it was going well—he enjoyed it.

The similarity of the male companionship of Vladimir and Estragon to a homosexual relationship is obvious to any audience, but critics and academics have avoided comment. Everything that might categorise a homosexual relationship is present except sex, and it is fairly obvious that the two tramps are almost certainly far past it. They have obviously been together for decades, and do not mention any women in their past. The relationship can symbolise any relationship between two people long accustomed to each other. Beckett himself has said that the two were like Suzanne and himself (their relationship will be mentioned later), intimating that they were a kind of marriage, but not in a conventional sense. In reality the pair were androgynous.

Homosexuality has been a taboo subject from Victorian times until the middle of the twentieth century. As it ceased to be a taboo an uneasiness has crept into male friendships that are not homosexual. Friendship has developed brakes and safeguards to remove suspicion that it could be something stronger, and this something applies where one member of a friendship is homosexual and the other not. At the same time the ambiguity of such a friendship can strengthen it, rather like friendships between men and women where for one reason or another sex is ruled out. Beckett grew up in a world where male friendships were perfectly normal (sex before marriage was extremely difficult) and he was the perfect male friend, a good companion, but he was aware of the changes in sexual mores—in prewar left-bank Paris he could hardly not be—and he simply ignored sexual inclination as something of no importance. He never had any need to prove his maleness or otherwise and his human warmth towards all his male friends of whatever persuasion showed no signs of either nuance or difference.

Vladimir and Estragon may therefore be homosexual or not. It makes no difference. They are two outcasts of society who find comfort in each other's company, as do Mercier and Camier, whose situation is less extreme. The relationship in each case is human companionship. It is different where a power element is present, as with Pozzo and Lucky and Hamm and Clov: here it is one of master and slave or servant. The most obvious man-woman relationship in Beckett's writing, other than the conventional Nagg and Nell in *Endgame*, is that of Winnie and Willie in *Happy Days*, which is ambiguous. Winnie in her ironic way loves Willie, and has no delusions about him, but it is not clear what his feelings are towards her: this is quite deliberate on the author's part. She is the stronger personality (the concept of Earth-Mother—Erda in German mythology—must have influenced Beckett's visual image, particularly in Wagner's very similar stage picture in the *Ring*), but she cannot move. Willie has mobility but little else. Does he hate her, for her fortitude, her nagging, or is he at the end, re-establishing a warmth, a companionship? When he reaches for the gun, is it to shoot her (perhaps out of compassion), or himself, or both? It has been a long stale marriage and Beckett leaves the audience to decide out of its own secret thoughts how the play should end.

Sex is an instant need and its durability in terms of desire is limited. Winnie's caustic comment to Willie on Aristotle's famous dictum regarding sexual love may be taken as a permanent, not a temporary sadness on Beckett's part. The joy of sex, for most of humanity, is very limited, and its portrayal in realistic, as against romantic images, is not stimulating to third parties. The couplings of Molloy with a number of women, who at times seem to be all the same with different names, or all different with optional names, contain little pleasure and joy. 'Twixt finger and thumb 'tis heaven in comparison.'[40] The little chambermaid he had once glimpsed, but never knew, is Molloy's fantasy image; that memory of her is what sex is all about for Molloy, unattainable as Beatrice was for Dante, which is the reference Beckett clearly had in mind. Molloy's real pleasure is masturbation, pleasure without consequence, and without the need to invade another person's privacy, and 'ideal' love has a place in it: but the lack of consequence is the real reason that the puritanical mind so disapproved of masturbation and the same reasoning or prejudice, is probably behind the most deep-seated foundations of homophobia. The contrast between 'ideal' and real-life love significantly emerges many times in Beckett's work and appears to be closely based on personal experience. The ideal is always unattainable

> Who loved could not be won
> Or won not loved
> or some other trouble[41]

What is too easily attainable is a relationship where the woman's demands in sexuality, time, attention and devotion, become more than an artist with his commitment to his art can entertain. And for a man, attractive to, and pursued by women, as Beckett was, the reaction was inevitably irritation, a desire to escape and a compression of all the different pursuing women into a single image:

They come
different and the same
with each it is different and the same
with each the absence of love is different
with each the desire of love is the same[42]

This has sometimes been taken to mean that Beckett was misogynistic and hated women. The opposite is true. He liked women very much, but feared their instinct for procreation and for devouring their mates.

Love as companionship is still very much love. It does not wax and wane as physical love does. It may have irritations, its quarrels, its disagreements, but unlike sexual love it is unlikely to turn into its opposite, hate. *Waiting for Godot* gives us a very realistic portrait of love as companionship, a bonding that will last as long as the protagonists survive. A male-female relationship that once was physical love can turn into that too: it is the natural progression for a couple, married or not, to become physically alienated in the sexual sense and then, with luck, friends. For this to happen there has to be a community of interests, attitudes and outlook. Such a bond is of course desirable, and it can become a very real panacea for the problems of ageing, incapability, illness and the other pains of life that become more acute with time. Such non-physical bonding is not however necessarily a social benefit to society, because there are many, if not more, anti-social bonded relationships as there are socially desirable ones. The solidarity of the higher social classes against the lower is one example. Many well-adjusted couples find their comfort and security in maintaining the class barrier; any similar political outlook also makes a strong bond, and this applies to religion as well. The more fanatically or fundamentally held a belief, prejudice, dogma or ideology is, the stronger the bond of those holding it. The essence of the philosophical, or scientific mind should be open-mindedness and scepticism, a willingness to be wrong and to change one's opinions in the face of evidence, but this can easily break or damage a bond between any two people or the members of a larger social group.

In *Waiting for Godot* Beckett tests out the bonding of companionship many times. Vladimir and Estragon agree and disagree without rancour. Pozzo shows himself to be open-minded up to a point, willing to consider a different opinion, but never to agree with it, a very Irish attitude. The bonding of Pozzo and Lucky is based, first on convenience, then on need, and although the roles are reversed—Lucky, the slave, although he has become dumb, is still mobile, while Pozzo, now blind, is totally dependent on him—the bond has grown stronger. Only because of it is Pozzo still the master; like Lear he has to count on the loyalty of the last of his servants. Hamm is basically the same character as Pozzo, blind at the beginning of *Endgame*, approaching his death with last-minute self-imposed dignity at the end. Although Clov is poised for departure and ready to leave him to his fate, he does not do so as long as the curtain is up, and the author leaves it to the audience to judge whether or not Clov will really depart. Each of us must test the bond and the loyalty in his mind, which may be stronger than the hate. Dogs do not often run away from bad masters.

Samuel Beckett won the Nobel Prize for Literature in 1969 because he was one of the few major writers, if not the first, to take as his subject matter the suffering of humanity and to make his principal characters the deprived, the persecuted and the exploited, a very large proportion of the human race living at any one time. He showed us what their lives are like, what went on inside their minds, how they try to cope and survive. It was not the way to win an easy audience: readers and theatre-goers either want to see their own lives reflected or to be able to vicariously enjoy the lives of others whom they would like to be, better off, more noble, more admirable in character. Like Dickens, Beckett strikes at the conscience, but he does not preach. He shows us things as they are, and although his models are the underside of society, we come to realise that however much better off we think we are, we are really all the same. In his celebrated 'vision' on the quayside at Dún Laoghaire, walking one black night in a tempest while his mother was approaching death in a nearby nursing home, he realised suddenly that his dark view of life and humanity, which he had been trying to push down, was in fact his greatest asset, and would convey his own individual message to the world and that from that vision he could find his own voice, and his signature as a creative artist.

By looking hard at blackness, one can begin to see a little light in 'the dimmest dim.'[43] When life seems bereft of any comfort it should be possible to find another, in similar or even worse circumstances, with whom to share one's misery, one's fears and apprehensions. Sharing makes the intolerable tolerable; it also makes us aware of the need to put a better face on things to cheer up the other, even if one thinks it is hopeless. Hopelessness discussed seems a little better. Beckett always looks at the very worst and then draws back a little. Above all, despair must be looked at directly and defied. The key word in his work may well be, as he claims, 'perhaps', but the last word he usually leaves us with is 'ON'. When everything else has been removed, one must still strive with a Promethean defiance, as long as the human will can function and retain consciousness, to go ON.

4

The Conquest of Time

Beckett's thoughts on time are complex and often seem contradictory, which is not surprising in a writer who had read so much and from so many sources, and whose own independent thinking was based on observation and imagination. As a young man of twenty-four he agreed to write a study of Proust, the writer who more than any other had made Time the principal hero of his major work; it was Beckett's first commercially published book. Before that he had won a £10 prize given by Nancy Cunard, one of the rich culture-loving ladies of the day, whose enthusiasm and taste for art was inevitably bound up with collecting and loving the talent that produced it. The prize was for a poem on the subject of time which had to be under a hundred lines. Hearing of it at the last moment Beckett spent a whole night writing *Whoroscope*, ninety-eight lines spoken by the philosopher Descartes, whose life by Adrien Baillet he had just finished reading.

Descartes is the father of modern philosophy. His system of rational thought starts from doubting everything except the premise that the individual thinks and therefore exists, and thus forcing his disciples and himself into extraordinary mental gymnastics, always taking the longest and most difficult route to establish a proof or even formulate a theory. This in itself recommended him to Beckett, a reluctant disbeliever as Descartes was a reluctant believer. Beckett's *Watt* is a brilliantly funny example of Cartesian reasoning in action where the author simultaneously admires and imitates the system and mocks the absurdities to which it can often lead. That everything has to be comprehended through the mind is obvious, but the ability of what is outside the mind to exist independently has occupied philosophers for the last three hundred years, not to speak of their Greek predecessors, and only Kant, whose prose is as convoluted as Descartes's is lucid, was able to build a system that would at least remain solid enough to become a platform for further wrestling.

To claim that time is the subject of the poem is to stretch the sense of the word, but Descartes was already at the end of his life at the period Beckett represents in his dramatic monologue; Descartes let no one know his exact age and he hid his birthday to prevent his horoscope from being cast; *Whoroscope* can then be said to be about the length and the quality of a life, the final accomplishment of the subject when near death, who is therefore 'complete' in Goethe's sense. There is no future, only a past. This looking back when near death is very Proustian, but Beckett was also to portray many of his future characters is a similar way, especially Molloy, Malone, Krapp and Hamm.

However much Beckett tries to look at the world objectively, the subjectivity of the human experience quickly intrudes. In *Whoroscope* the old Descartes, working as house philosopher to Queen Christina of Sweden, who forced him to rise at five in the morning to attend on her (whereas his lifelong habit had been to stay in bed until noon), thus making him the subject of much court jealousy and intrigue, was not a happy man, but he was still working on philosophical problems, knowing his death could not be far off. Time was for him the little of it that remained.

Proust was published a year after *Whoroscope* and it tells us much more about its author than about the subject: it is a critical study of much significance to those interested in Beckett in that it lets us into its author's mind at the time, and into his stream of thought and preoccupations, revealing the wealth and breadth of his reading, and it does so more directly than any of his other writings, except perhaps the *Duthuit Dialogues*. It is marred at times by over-cleverness, a tendency to show off, that Beckett did not wholly overcome until after the war. The long essay really consists of his own thoughts on the human predicament expressed through his analysis of the philosophy and literary accomplishment of Marcel Proust.

In his first paragraph he defines time as a 'double-headed

monster of damnation and salvation'. He goes on to describe the stages by which Proust threw away the conventions of space and sequence to describe an age and a society differently and more intimately than had been possible before, and quotes a famous passage from the end of *A la Recherche du temps perdu*, in his own translation:

> But were I granted time to accomplish my work, I would not fail to stamp it with the seal of that Time, now so forcibly present to my mind, and in it I would describe men, even at the risk of giving them the appearance of monstrous beings, as occupying in Time a much greater place than that so sparingly conceded to them in Space, a place indeed extended beyond measure, because, like giants plunged in the years, they touch at once those periods of their lives—separated by so many days—so far apart in Time.[44]

An hour glass is often used symbolically to denote the passage of time, but Beckett comes up with a better image:

> The individual is the seat of a constant process of decantation, decantation from the vessel containing the fluid of future time, sluggish, pale and monochrome, to the vessel containing the fluid of past time, agitated and multicoloured by the phenomena of its hours.[45]

Our tendency is to look at the past with a combination of nostalgia, where even dramatically unpleasant incidents take on greater interest in retrospect than they had at the time when they were often a source of anxiety and pain, and causality, as if the past had been a period of education and experience that formed us into what we have become up to the present, the classic literary example being Goethe's theory of the *Bildungsroman* in which characters become the totality of everything they have experienced. In this view we are only complete at the moment of our demise. We tend not to look ahead in realistic terms, but 'in the haze of our smug will to live, of our pernicious and incurable optimism'.[46] The fluid of future time that will be decanted is correspondingly colourless and without any characteristic at all, the opposite of the vividness of past time. The future only troubles us when, as in the case of Faust, a menace lies in wait on the calendar, a date that will certainly arrive, when we have an appointment with some event that will break the habit of day succeeding day with little change, be it a wedding, a court case, a career decision, an operation, or the arrival of the grim reaper. Suddenly we realise that we cannot control the future: it is the great unknown of boundless possibilities. We become aware, as Beckett puts it, of the bitterness of fatality (even for what on the surface might seem to be a happy forthcoming event) and of what 'is in store for us, not in store in us.'[47]

Memory and habit are interlinked. The nostalgia for the past has become part of our mind-set and we build our everyday existence on habit; even pain and illness can become habit. Habit is also linked to the future, but in a different way; for habit is a treaty between the individual and his external world, the perception of which occupies so large a part in the philosophy discussed in Chapter 2. The world is constantly changing, and so is our response to it, and that of our habits.

We also become a different person or series of different persons as time passes. Life becomes a succession of habits because the individual is a succession of individuals, having more or less memory of what it was like to be his or her own previous self. Some try to overcome habit by living dangerously, and they incur the inevitable risks while losing the security of the deadening qualities that are part of habit. Beckett here quotes Leopardi to underline his point that 'wisdom consists not in the satisfaction but in the ablation of desire,'[48] an attitude he had earlier absorbed from Geulinex. However, for Beckett there is no particular significance in how one lives or deals with habit: the pain of living cannot be avoided, it can at best be reduced. To be set in your ways, or to operate outside them does not make you a different person. A change of behaviour is in any case unlikely to have much effect on outside events.

Proust, as seen by Beckett, divides time up into segments, each representing a change in the personality and mental growth of the individual, corresponding to a change in his personality and intellectual development. This, in turn, corresponds to a change in his habit formation, or more exactly of the contractual arrangement between the individual mind and the external world. The knowledge that one is undergoing a constant loss of past identity and in the process acquiring a partial new one is troubling to the person who values his present consciousness enough to want it not to change, and the normal resistance to new ideas is a reflection of this. We accept our past personalities but not the unknown future ones. And our changing emotions, such as the diminution with time of grief at a death, or a failure to love with the same ardour as previously, is also painful to contemplate. This is the effect that habit has on consciousness (memory) through time.

Time is individualised objectively and any time outside the individual human experience becomes something else, closer to space than time, because it exists outside human perception. But of course, our increasing knowledge of space also increases our concept of time and the two become linked, even at times interchangeable, because we understand distance increasingly in terms of time.

But as time is subjective to the human mind it is also elastic. Proust covers great acres of time in a very few pages and then uses hundreds of pages to describe a very small time-frame of events. Memory is selective and releases us from time's tyranny by allowing us to regain it, reliving selected events many times over. Robbe-Grillet borrows Proustian time in his first novel *Un Régicide*, where his protagonist relives an embarrassing incident repeatedly, unable to halt the mental loop that brings him back to the beginning again each time his memory, more and more vivid with shame, returns to the point where the incident starts. So do we all relive our triumphs and failures, perhaps giving some events a different turning in imagination.

Time, habit and memory between them become a three-headed monster, almost a divine one, containing the essence of the problem posed and, in their unison, the possible solution. Memory is most potent when it is involuntary, the most banal little incident, perhaps a long-lost habit, like Proust's famous madeleine, the taste of which dipped into tea brings back a whole lost paradise of childhood, suddenly becoming the most important sensation in the mind. It is the principle of Pavlov's conditioned reflex. A musical tune, a passage in a book, a sight seen again or bringing to mind a similar sight, can recall a whole past world by an accidental act of perception, almost one of 'intellectual animism'.[49]

Proust had a bad memory and that is why it is so interesting. A good memory cannot be very interesting because there is no contrast between what is significant and what not. Everything can be recalled, and therefore there is no sense of discovery. Perception is the trigger of memory and if nothing is forgotten there is nothing to be triggered; it is already all there on the surface. What we contain in our minds and will want eventually, but unknowingly, to recall, is put there by accident, or as Beckett evidently believes, by instinct: it has been registered by our extreme inattention at the time and 'stored in that ultimate and inaccessible dungeon of our being to which Habit does not possess the key.'[50] What Beckett is saying is that we can build and store within the unconscious a secret garden that can be evoked by an association or an accidental recognition, either a *déjà vu* (or *entendu* or *senti*), or the sense of wonder on seeing something new but familiar, as if it were remembered from a previous life, or from a dream, or at any rate from something outside everyday experience and reality. His point is that 'this is the best of our many selves',[51] that it contains whatever might be divine in our essence. It is the escape from the everyday with its depressing realities, above all from its habits, into a form of Joycean epiphany. It may be only momentary, but it is all the more significant for that. Habit is the enemy of that epiphany, that moment when we temporarily escape from the determinism of life. In time it is brief, but it may be conjured up again. And it is time, and probably space as well, that separates it—the moment of recall—from the hidden treasures, stored away waiting to be discovered, *not* rediscovered, for the moment of recall and experiencing again is not the same as the original experience which will have had no importance at the time. It is later that one realises the value of what has been lost, and that 'the carapace of paste and pewter'[52] is in fact a pearl.

Although Beckett is interpreting Proust, it is not difficult to discern from the heightening of lyricism in his language, that he has identified himself with the Proustian discovery, linked it to Joyce, and added it to his own armoury of philosophical spears with which to attack the 'great deadener' as he was later to call Habit in Vladimir's monologue, which he elsewhere seems to advocate as one prescription for 'the ablation of desire'.[53] Another way of looking at it is to say that there is no contradiction, that ablation is not intended to reduce suffering, but to accompany it in a self-negating acceptance of spiritual and actual poverty. This would seem to be supported by his image of involuntary memory as 'an immediate, total and delicious deflagration',[54] presumably a Proustian quotation, which I have not been able to trace as Beckett does not give his sources, which has a magical power and is uncontrollable; but such moments contain the backward metamorphoses of life when we stop being our present personality and go back to another, earlier self. The link between the two, in space and in time, is an Euclidean line of the personality one often finds later in Beckett, especially when there is an appearance, or reported appearance, of a boy (denoting youth with its years of suffering still ahead), linking the various old men of Beckett's post-war writing to their younger selves, and simultaneously to the future, to a continuity of humanity. In this case it is the line that links the old Proust to his childhood madeleine soaked in tea, the key to his great novel, in the same way as a sleigh, the *Rosebud*, was later to become the key to Orson Welles' film *Citizen Kane*.

The natural conclusion to Proust's conception of the past living in the involuntary memory of the present is, as Beckett sees it, both that the past is superior and that the dead can live again. So Proust had to be able to bring his grandmother 'living and complete' back to life, totally in his mind and memory before he was able to realise the full impact of her death. Here again Proust's genius explains an everyday familiar phenomenon in a way that is instantly understandable to those who have never grasped how the reality of a death sinks in slowly. Beckett's essay on Proust appears to be the first time that he himself had examined the continuing life of the dead through the memories of others: this was soon to become an important image and *Leitmotif* in his work. From it he developed his 'Voices', hovering over the living and the charnel house of the world, in some Dantean limbo or purgatory, reviewing their past lives, and also the series of ghosts of the later work, bringing together that potent cocktail, memory and imagination. The image of the young Proust's grandmother, knowing she was dying, wanting to be remembered, not as a *disease* (from which she would die) but as a grandmother allowing herself to be carefully photographed so that her picture will remind Marcel one day of her existence in his early years, is more accurately etched into his memory than the photograph itself in its silver frame. Ultimately past time becomes more real than present time, a place of escape, of pleasure, of seeming greater significance. The past is real, the present too subjective to be characterised, except in terms of the colourless liquid of the future pouring through it into the past.

The measuring of time requires a measuring standard, and the most convenient for us is the biblical length of a life, seventy years. Beckett was very much aware of that biblical average, especially as few in his family had achieved it. Krapp, as near to an *alter ego* of the author as he allowed himself to create, is sixty-nine and expecting soon to die. I had dinner with Beckett shortly before his seventieth birthday, and commenting on the coming watershed, he said; 'Seventy, that's old age! When you're old the only thing left is work. Work must be your company.' And that is what he entitled the book he was finishing at the time, perhaps the most successful of the late texts with his public.

In *Company* the narrator is lying flat on his back, lost in his own mind, hearing a voice, and aware of a second voice, but it is soon obvious that all the voices are really his own. What enlivens this otherwise fairly forbidding text are the considerable number of biographical vignettes, memories from childhood and young adulthood, one even from the day of his birth, that are extremely touching and vivid. In essence, *Com-*

pany is a collection of life memories that catch special moments in terms of Proustian inadvertent memories, but it does not try to measure time: one is only aware of the timelessness of the thinking mind. The significance of the childhood memories, like those of Proust, is that these are the only *real* moments of life, the moments that can contain a certain notion of happiness, seen in retrospect, because the protagonist at the time was concerned with his hopeful future, but, of course, the future never comes. Happiness has to be in the immediate present—and such moments in a lifetime are inevitably rare and of short duration—or in the golden past, coloured in the future present as it never can be at the time. Happiness is possible in the course of a life, but really only when it is already in the past. Present happiness, if one is aware of it, is really a celebration of some event that has just been accomplished: this could be some career triumph or a successful sexual coupling, but as soon as one is aware of being happy the reason for it has ended, and the sensation of happiness is already fading, like that of the Beckett boy in the story of the hedgehog in *Company*, whose glow at having accomplished a good deed fades slowly as he ponders its consequences, and then turns into a great unease. In recall, happiness, already feeling the sense of loss that follows the euphoric moment, is not a condition. It is a past moment lighting up the present. In talking of happiness, a brief, temporary state of mind, I am not in any way referring to contentment, which is different and passive: contentment is an acceptance of what exists, whereas happiness is focused on a moment or a series of moments of exceptional significance.

Life's journey is compared by Proust to passing a series of vases, each containing a perfume, suspended along the line (his word is height) of our progress through time and space. The vases wait for the moment of our passing, then some accidental event, such as the triggering of an association by stumbling on a cobblestone, will release the perfume and create an epiphany. We are not aware of the vases, nor of the moment when the perfume will strike our nostrils, but when it happens 'we breathe the true air of Paradise, of the only Paradise that is not the dream of a madman, the Paradise that has been lost.'[55] Fifteen years later much of this was to re-emerge in the sub-text of *Godot*, a play primarily about time, as are all Beckett's plays in a sense, but none more so than the work which brought him world success and acclaim, as well as much opposite hostile reaction.

Beckett's image of future time decanting itself into past time is one of time running backward; the future is in constant flow into the past, the opposite of our normal perception. What is it that flows forward then? It can only be our consciousness which we tend to confuse with time because it perceives it. As time and consciousness move in different directions they can be seen as a series of collisions, and that surely is the best way to describe the immediate present, the present moment: as the confrontation of time moving backward and consciousness moving forward. Beckett never says this directly, but it is the logical conclusion to his philosophically poetic reasoning. The waiting vases, each a memory prepared to be evoked by consciousness moving forward, are passed at the moment when future time encounters consciousness. It is the future that blends present and past at the moment of decantation. As we wait for the future, the past gets longer, the future shorter, at least in terms of personal consciousness. Although we have the impression that we are moving forward, we are in practice waiting for the future all our lives in a present that is like the swirling waters of two tides flowing into each other. It is no accident that Beckett's interest in time led to a new perception of waiting.

The situation in *Waiting for Godot* is one of waiting, as Beckett himself had to wait for most of the war years at Roussillon, in the same countryside that is described in the play. Vladimir's time is not the time of a life, but of a day, or else of the duration of the wait until Godot comes to 'save' the two of them, or of the time until their patience is exhausted and they look for some other solution. The time of Pozzo is measured by his decisions and his circumstances, and probably consists of the time between his departure and his return to his manor. Those at the bottom of the human heap always have to measure time in shorter spaces than those at the top. The time of Pozzo is therefore longer than the duration of the play. All these measurements of time are subjective and stretch from watershed to watershed.

For the slave-philosopher Lucky, time is not subjective, but measured as the time of human existence. His 'think' contains not so much a philosophy as, in embryo, the synthesis of Beckett's most profound convictions about the nature of our relationship, and that of any divine or controlling power, to the whole structure of being and the future of mankind. Lucky is the modern equivalent of one of Shakespeare's wise fools, a madman who utters profound truths. There are three themes in his *think*, which is not an argument but a conviction, closely linked to his desire to end his own miserable existence. The first is the indifference of Heaven—and of a God that faces in all directions at once—to mankind and the sufferings of the world. We can link this to the manicheist belief, which much interested Beckett, that God is at a great distance from the world, indifferent to and possibly even unaware of our existence, while it is the Devil that rules the world. The second theme is that man wastes and pines (in spite of better nutrition and engaging in healthy activities such as sport: the momentous and the casual are combined and interwoven in Lucky's speech) and will eventually die out as a species, as much from the neglect of God as from his own stupidity and innate destructiveness.

Beckett's wartime experiences will certainly have contributed to this part of the monologue. And the third is the cooling of the earth, the great cold, when the planet will become an empty abode of stones, with the remains of mankind, perhaps a few skulls, still lying on its surface. The great cooling and the end of all life is suggested elsewhere in Beckett's work, in *Endgame* particularly, where the end would seem to be not far off. The earliest version of this play made it clear that what Beckett had in mind when he was writing it was an earlier destruction of the world, the great flood, survived only by Noah (Hamm is, of course, a biblical name, one of Noah's sons), and Hamm's fear is that the growth of the human species will start all over again, which in Genesis, it does. *Lessness* refers to a great catastrophe as if the last survivors on earth were gasping their last breaths, and in *Ill Seen Ill Said*, to which I shall return in Chapter 7, there are references to stones encroaching irreversibly on the earth's vegetation. The final extinction of man, not such a bad thing as it will end all suffering, is an ever-present probability underlying Beckett's thought, and the resonances invade nearly all his work.

Time in *Waiting for Godot* is different for each of the characters; even between Vladimir and Estragon there is a difference: Estragon wants to eat when he is hungry, but Vladimir can wait, knowing that hunger will be worse later, and he can remember much better what happened yesterday, while his friend neither remembers nor cares. But each knows very well what time is ultimately about, it is the time between now and death. There is little in their past to bring back by a Proustian association. There is a dim memory of coloured maps of the Holy Land in a child's book of Bible stories, some recollection of things read or heard. Pozzo, no doubt, has much to remember, but he has become an old man in the last act, and he too is looking towards his end. Only Lucky seems to have more to say about the past and he is now dumb, his reasoning powers and philosophical memories, as well as his vengeful hopes for the end of all his tormentors, locked in his head. Vladimir already sees the future, a barren earth, because he can see the charnel house beneath his feet, the corpses of all those who have preceded him gone into the ground, whose voices he fancies he can hear in the air. This is pure Beckett, not Proust. And here habit is everything, a means to surviving a little longer, by inventing rituals, playing games, continuing to hope, above all trying to find a way to be remembered, so that all the past and present does not become a quickly forgotten waste in the great wastage of human existence.

And what is death but an emancipation from time? That is of course only on condition that death really means death, not an entry into another consciousness or another sphere. For Proust, the only real escape from life was into art and, through unexpected memory, into the golden moments of the past, always yielding a magic that is impossible in the present. But for Beckett even art was not enough. He saw it as a trap to turn our eyes away from the realities of life and the true horror of our predicament: facing the horror was for him the only way to be really alive.

5

The Failure of Art

It is hard to imagine anyone with a surer instinct for art than Samuel Beckett. He had a mind that was able to grasp the essence of an art work, whatever its discipline or its complexity of style, at first encounter. Had he wished to be a painter, a composer or, like Breton, an *animateur* and leader of a school of artists as well as a writer, he would have been at least as successful. His talent was like a precious metal that can be shaped in many different ways. His eccentricity as a young writer would have been accepted as quite normal had he been a painter, and although there are few eminent composers who were near contemporaries (Messaien and Shostakovitch, each an individualist, are two names that spring to mind), his date of birth, occurring between that of those who created the avant-garde expressionism of the second Vienna school, and those later musicians one associates with surrealism and its contemporary movements, we have it on the evidence of Marcel Mihalovici, with whom he collaborated over the operatic version of *Krapp's Last Tape*, that he had all the musical talent that was needed to be a successful composer. Those who have seen him at the piano know that he was as consummate a musician as someone who never practised could be. In fact it was music that troubled him most, because he understood it so well. He would not allow himself to love it fully, because the emotional force of music, as he well knew, can be overpowering and distracting to someone as sensitive to it as he was. The resemblance of his dramatic structures and much of his writing to music has received considerable comment, and the reason that the many attempts to set his poems to music have never yet really succeeded—the poems have always done more for the music than the other way round—is because music is already so obviously there in the cadences and the rhythms.

Beckett became a writer of a philosophical nature, creating art against his will, because he wanted to understand meaning, and he knew that art, the greatest of all escapes from the mundane world for an intellectual, is the biggest obstacle to finding the plain unvarnished truth that his Protestant, agnostic nature drove him to find. A religious mystic, whose whole being is infused with the love of God, based on awe and self-loathing, has a single idea: to enter Heaven and to spend eternity looking at God directly and to become lost in the wonder of that contemplation. Beckett's driving desire was to look at the full horror of the situation into which God (or whatever the cause of our suffering can be called) has put us, and to realise it fully and absolutely with nothing to deflect that gaze. He also needed, out of anger and his understanding of what our invisible enemy has done, to make some gesture, however puny, against that evil power. This could only consist of doing something impossible, but the *will* of man (and this concept he took directly from Schopenhauer) is capable of doing something extraordinary, even impossible at times, in other words, it can accomplish a kind of miracle. Such a gesture may well be pointless, but it is an action taken against the determinism of our situation, and our view of his writing can be just that, determination.

Beckett has said repeatedly that all he ever wanted to do was to put his head against the cliff-rock and push until he had moved it a fraction of a millimetre further away. It would be enough just to defy God, as Prometheus did Zeus, when he stole the sacred fire from heaven for the benefit of mankind; to be punished for it eternally would be worthwhile. The paradox lies in the method, Art itself, which to Beckett was also the hindrance. He saw art as an encumbrance, a deflection from a will that should be concentrated entirely on hating God. Some of the catastrophes that God visits on us may even be seen as a challenge. We are all victims, but the depth of our affliction does not always allow us to return the venom as we would like.

> He will curse God again as in the blessed days face to the open sky the passing deluge. Little body grey face features crack and

little holes two pale blue. Blank planes sheer white eye calm long last all gone from mind.[56]

For Proust art was ultimately everything, the only activity that could make life possible. For the non-artist, of course, it is habit that plays that role. Pointing out that it is through Time, in its creative and destructive aspects, that Proust discovered himself as an artist, Beckett quotes a famous phrase: 'I understood the meaning of death, of love and vocation, of the joys of the spirit and the utility of pain.'[57] Beckett never wrote anything about Kafka, almost certainly because at the time when he was reading and analysing other writers as well as philosophers, Kafka was not yet known to the outside world. His international fame only began after 1945, but Beckett knew and admired his work, in so many ways closer to his own than Proust's.[58] The sense of one's smallness and unimportance in a big, confusing, unknowable world, and of self-disgust at one's own inadequacy, is common to both writers, but Kafka's response is passive, while Beckett's attitude is Promethean. Both sent out probes to the space beyond man's understanding, in Kafka's case trying to find meaning by following the strings of cause and consequence backwards and forwards to see where they lead, seeking to make sense out of the confusion of everything, only to find that the strings lead nowhere. Beckett's probes also never reach their destination, but he only shows them travelling, possibly into infinity, like Zeno's arrow, always moving and always still. The journeys of man, as seen by Beckett, are fruitless and break down as the mind recedes into its own depth and fading consciousness. But the similarity of outlook, atmosphere and pessimism between Beckett and Kafka will always link them together in the history of literature. Art for Kafka was the most beautiful thing imaginable, something that was not quite attainable, too good for himself, highly desirable, but more attainable by others, an attitude supremely Jewish. For Beckett, art was everything that is most desirable and therefore to be feared more than anything else. He did not have a love-hate for art, but a love-fear.

And at the same time he was himself not only an artist, but

the very prototype of an artist. Art was his world, the only field in which he could possibly work with any validity. His friends were artists or, if not professionally in the arts, belonging in all important respects to that world. Beckett knew that all creativity is a form of vanity, but the artist cannot stop himself being creative, and it is in the *Duthuit Dialogues* that he best explains his dilemmas and theories of art.

These remarkable dialogues purport to be his memories of discussions, sitting in cafés while playing chess with Georges Duthuit, an art critic who after the war had taken over Eugène Jolas's English-language magazine *Transition*, in the pre-war era the most distinguished publication of its kind. There was no connection other than the name between the two periodicals, the latter appearing in French, but by acquiring the right to continue, Duthuit was able to get an allowance of that extremely scarce commodity, paper. Duthuit, a man of taste and learning, had a fairly conventional view of art, especially of the plastic arts, a subject which Beckett, because of his many painter friends, was well qualified to discuss. The dialogues, written down subsequently from memory are highly stylised, obviously condensing many discussions into three, each built around a painter, but each with a field of argument that went well beyond painting. Beckett's aesthetic, although found puzzling by many people, is always clearly expressed and in language of great lucidity and poetic beauty.

The first, the shortest, is devoted to Tal Coat (pronounced Coh-At), a French painter (1905–1985) whose reputation has not grown bigger with the years. But the painter is of little importance in the dialogue. The point made by Beckett is that this avant-garde figure of the day, going a little further into abstraction than his predecessor, probing a little further into the unknown, was simply carrying a relay-torch. Continuing a tradition and furthering it was, for him, not enough.

> What we have to consider in the case of Italian painters is not that they surveyed the world with the eyes of building-contractors, a mere means like any other, but that they never stirred from the field of the possible, however much they may have enlarged it.[59]

When Duthuit asks what art can possibly do other than to work 'on the plane of the feasible', do what is possible in the circumstances and through the means available in one's own time, Beckett quickly comes back:

> Logically, none. Yet I speak of an art turning from it in disgust, weary of puny exploits, weary of pretending to be able, of being able, of doing a little better the same old thing, of going a little further along a dreary road.
> — And preferring what?
> — The expression that there is nothing to express, nothing with which to express, no power to express, no desire to express, together with the obligation to express.[60]

Beckett at this point has ceased to argue, and has moved far away from the peg of Tal Coat on which they have been hanging their critical coats, stepping sideways to express his objection to the role of art as it is commonly seen, either presenting a view of the world or providing decoration, in which the artist, for the sake of his own ego, and to advance his career, tries to move the art of painting a little further forward, rather as Beckett saw himself wanting to push the rock face another millimetre away. It is a means of individual expression, of vanity and of living in the world, to Beckett a surrender to compulsion, and to the acceptance of art as a panacea for living. But at the same time the artist cannot stop himself. His is the same role as that of the female giving birth, unable to control the forces of her own nature, and Beckett was well aware of the comparison. The *obligation to express* is sadly outside the artist's control. The alternative to accepting the obligation to express is total surrender to apathy, which Beckett sometimes advocated and often claimed was his own situation, but his output proves the contrary. In the end he *expressed* because he was unable not to do so.

Masson is the painter who is ostensibly the subject of the second dialogue. Here the argument is largely on the dilemma of the artist, aware of his own inadequacy in the great field of art, and the great unknown to be explored that is the world, striving nonetheless to overcome that inadequacy and to paint something that will 'frolic among the focusless fields (we are talking of abstract, non-representational painting), tumultuous with incessant creation.'[61] The words are supposed to be Duthuit's, quoting the painter. Beckett, however, is far more interested in having the painter simply accept his inadequacy, which is that of every artist, because in no way is he denying Masson's merit. He, Beckett, dreams of an art that is purely imaginary, leaving nothing for the viewer outside his own mind, in other words, no art at all. But he also leaves the last word to his opponent, and allows him to put (in Beckett's very beautiful words) the whole argument for art to exist at all as a joyous counterweight to the misery of the world:

> . . . must we really deplore the painting that admits 'the things and creatures of spring, resplendent with desire and affirmation, ephemeral no doubt, but immortally reiterant', not in order to enjoy them, but in order that what is tolerable and radiant in the world may continue? Are we really to deplore the painting that is a rallying, among the things of time that pass and hurry us away, towards a time that endures and gives increase?[62]

I repeat, that although the argument as Beckett remembered it is Duthuit's, the words are those of the author, who, unable to answer, at the end, *exits weeping*! One is reminded of Kafka's last conversation with Max Brod, when in reply to the latter's protestation that there had to be some hope for the future, answered, 'Yes, perhaps, but not for us.'

But it is in the last and longest dialogue, where the subject is Beckett's friend Bram van Velde, who probably owes his subsequent reputation mainly to his connection with the author, where Beckett gives us the full blast of his objection to art. Here too he allows himself to be beaten, as at chess (which he probably usually won during these discussions, being an excellent player), by recognising that his outlook is logically unacceptable in the context of a society trying to improve itself and make life more tolerable for more people. Beckett recognised physical poverty, the condition of most of his heroes, but considered it as nothing compared to spiritual poverty. Nevertheless he often uses one as a metaphor for the other. He did not want an art that made life more tolerable, or anything that might deflect the human gaze from the full realisation of its own horror. One cannot build an argument to support such a view, which is profoundly emotional and grounded in a Promethean (a word I shall not use again) defiance of whatever lies behind the creation of the human race.

At no point in these dialogues, and certainly not in the last one, must one take the general points made about the attitudes of the painters too seriously. Their great talent, right or wrong, is taken for granted and attitudes are foisted onto them. When Beckett says that van Velde is helpless and 'cannot paint. . .is unable to act, acts, in the event paints, since he is obliged to paint,'[63] he is describing himself. Beckett's archetypal artist does not know why he has to practice his art, and can see no possible subject for art to tackle or any means for creation to take place. Artists do what they do, as well as they can, all the same. Beckett, after much cogitation and hesitation, finally declares that art, at least in the present context, is inexpressive. Expression is a tie: the escape from it must be total, in essence it is total impotence, and as such, a new kind of art of nothingness. Although there is more than an element of tongue-in-cheek in the dialogues, and the magnificence of the prose and the choice of metaphors make them very entertaining to read, Beckett underneath it all is deadly serious, making wonderful points that were totally shocking to the optimistic post-war period when they were written, and are still shocking to those of his readers and audiences today who view him as a great poetical manipulator of new language to be enjoyed, quoted and wallowed in, but who would have great difficulty, being art-lovers, in accepting his premise that art should take no form, but remain only a concept in the mind, and that it is metaphorically an invention of the Devil to deceive us into seeing life in rather rosier terms. The following two quotations are necessary to demonstrate this.

'. . .Let us, for once, be foolish enough not to turn tail. All have turned wisely tail, before the ultimate penury, back to the mere misery where destitute virtuous mothers may steal bread for their starving brats. There is more than a difference of degree between being short, short of the world, short of self, and being without these esteemed commodities. The one is a predicament, the other not.'

'. . . There are many ways in which the thing I am trying in vain to say may be tried in vain to be said. I have experimented, as you know, both in public and in private, under duress, through faintness of heart, through weakness of mind, with two or three hundred. The pathetic antithesis possession-poverty was perhaps not the most tedious. But we begin to weary of it, do we not? The realisation that art has always been bourgeois, although it may dull our pain before the achievements of the socially progressive, is finally of scant interest. The analysis of the relation between the artist and his occasion, a relation always regarded as indispensable, does not seem to have been very productive either, the reason being perhaps that it lost its way in disquisitions on the nature of occasion. It is obvious that for the artist obsessed with his expressive vocation, anything and everything is doomed to become occasion, including, as is apparently to some extent the case with Masson, the pursuit of occasion, and the every man his own wife experiments of the spiritual Kandinsky. No painting is more replete than Mondrian's. But if the occasion appears as an unstable term of relation, the artist, who is the other term, is hardly less so, thanks to his warren of modes and attitudes. The objections to this dualist view of the creative process are unconvincing. Two things are established, however precariously: the aliment, from fruits on plates to low mathematics and self-commiseration, and its manner of dispatch. All that should concern us is the acute and increasing anxiety of the relation itself, as though shadowed more and more darkly by a sense of invalidity, of inadequacy, of existence at the expense of all that it excludes, all that it blinds to. The history of painting, here we go again, is the history of the attempts to escape from this sense of failure, by means of more authentic, more ample, less exclusive relations between representer and representee, in a kind of tropism towards a light as to the nature of which the best opinions continue to vary, and with a kind of Pythagorean terror, as though the irrationality of pi were an offence against the deity, not to mention his creature. My case, since I am in the dock, is that van Velde is the first to desist from the estheticised automatism, the first to submit wholly to the incoercible absence of relation, in the absence of terms or, if you like, in the presence of unavailable terms, the first to admit that to be an artist is to fail, as no other dare fail, that failure is his world and the shrink from it desertion, art and craft, good housekeeping, living. No, no allow me to expire. I know that all that is required now, in order to bring even this horrible matter to an acceptable conclusion, is to make of this submission, this admission, this fidelity to failure, a new occasion, a new form of relation, and of the act which, unable to act, obliged to act, he makes, an expressive act, even if only of itself, of the impossibility, of its obligation. I know that my inability to do so places myself, and perhaps an innocent, in what I think is still called an unenviable situation, familiar to psychiatrists . . .

That, quoted almost in full, is Beckett's longest single statement on his own aesthetic. It is prefaced by his saying that he intended to say what the artist in question thinks he does, after which he will say what he really does. The second statement is never made, Beckett getting out of it, by declaring that he was mistaken in whatever point he wanted to make. The most significant lines are those given above where he talks of the necessary failure of art, ('that failure is his world'). On the one hand this is a statement that would be echoed by almost every major artist down the centuries; no writer, painter or composer of the first rank has ever been satisfied with his accomplishment; and that satisfaction is left to those well below the first rank, whose egos are greater than their talent. But that is not the way that the art-loving public feels about its favourite artists, being unable to glimpse the artist's dream, always just out of reach. Beckett, however, is doing more than voicing the dissatisfaction of artists with their own limitations.

Art for him is not a part of life, a human activity, a means of earning a living, of self-expression. It is the act of creation itself. The making of the world and the making of a painting differ only in scale. The hatred of the creator of all things can therefore be transferred to the mortal artist. Man may have invented God in his own image, and if so he has invented a very imperfect God, easy to hate for the malignity of his handiwork. But modern conceptions of God become ever more abstract, like modern paintings, and like much modern art they fail to convince anyone other than those who conceive them. God may congratulate himself, but no thinking, feeling member of humanity is likely to do so. The God that is worshipped in churches is a very small God, portrayed like a king, in essence like an authoritarian man who enjoys being wor-shipped, praised for the accidental good things around us that are most noticeable, and never blamed for the multiple evils of the world. If God has any resemblance to a man, it surely has to be that of an artist and therefore the artist is culpable. He should slink around in guilt: Beckett did.

6

Philosophy and Language

The role of language is much more important in the work of Samuel Beckett than in that of almost any other writer, even Joyce. The fact that he wrote in two, English and French, and English for an Irish writer means, in any case, confronting two uses of the same language, is only partially significant. Even before the war he had changed the possibilities of language by developing his own, very personal style to give a view of human behaviour, sometimes dispassionately, more often with vivid human description, and sardonically bitter humour, containing the casual acceptance of everyday disaster and cruelty, that so accurately reflects the way people really think and behave, and not the way they think they do. When he switched to French he developed his own, first very pure and later more revolutionary use of the language, and when he began translating himself back into English, it was to innovate further, less eccentrically, but with increased impact. Above all he weeded out, in the later work, any superfluous implantations, thereby achieving a prose of maximum economy where adjectives were sparingly used and anything in the present time of the speaker that was not within eyeshot or hearing would not be present, except as memory.

But aside from his technical development of new language as a vehicle for his thought, breaking up the structure of sentences to impart new patterns of imagery and speech into bumpy jumps of consciousness that superposed surprising associations and his personal codification into the stream of narrative, there is also, buried in the text, a system of undermeanings that only close reading can bring out. So, for instance, when Beckett uses a 'dead' language, especially Latin, it is usually to imply that death is lurking underneath the prose. Beckett's widespread use of unfamiliar words, often of terms that have gone out of use, or where only one side of its meaning is still employed, often creating neologisms out of the logic of words themselves, or deriving their opposite meaning by seeking the contrary sense of a word in use, not only helps to create new language, but new thought patterns as well.

So for instance in *More Pricks than Kicks*, Belacqua scoffs at the idea of a *sequitur* from his body to his mind.[64] Whereas we hear of *non sequiturs*, especially in philosophy, a *sequitur* is not an easy word to find in a dictionary, even in a Latin dictionary, although its derivation from *sequor* (following) makes its meaning not difficult to deduce; Beckett's use of *Félo-de-se*, the little used Latin term for suicide, crops up in *Murphy* at the inquest. This inspired Aidan Higgins, something of a Beckett protégé in his youth, to name his first book of short stories with that title, thereby extending its usage. Christopher Ricks[65] appears to be the first to have realised that when Beckett uses Latin, or other dead or semi-dead languages, his subject matter is never very far from human death. Beckett has encoded much of his philosophical thinking in little-known words by searching them out, as well as using outdated phrases and expressions, mainly, but not always, in his two principal languages, English and French. This, no doubt, necessitated much study of dictionaries and reference books. Bertrand Russell's claim that 'by means of study of syntax, we can arrive at considerable knowledge concerning the structure of the world'[66] applies to no one more than Beckett. He reshapes sentence structure, punctuation and word association. He uses arcane words to hide thoughts that are often not very palatable to readers who enjoy his wit and way with words, but balk at his insights into human cruelty and are alarmed by the preoccupation with death and darkness. What is hidden in the codes can be shared by his close readers, those willing to look up the rare words and their meanings, and to decipher the logic of his semineologisms like Belaqua's '*sequitur*'.

When Beckett wants to portray life in terms of its absurdity, its illogicality, its meaninglessness, he does it through a great rush of language, juxtaposing the familiar and the unfamiliar.

I think of these outbursts as rather like operatic arias. It is impossible to stop these heightened moments in their momentum by consulting dictionaries and reference books at the same time, without spoiling the pleasure of the text itself. Arsene's 'short statement' in *Watt* is a good example of this, although there the arcanenesses are limited, and there are none in Mr. Madden's speech in *Mercier and Camier*. But Lucky's much shorter speech is full of strange references. The audience is not meant to understand them: it is up to its most interested members to look up what they have missed afterwards, when they have obtained the text. And then the information and the message gradually become known to those who are really interested. Learning about the operas of a complex composer such as Wagner is very similar.

Beckett's fondness for language games is not merely an indulgence, a means of amusing himself, in line with his stated dictum that words have always been his principal love. They are, in fact, a form of healing. Like Wittgenstein, Beckett believed that philosophy is a personal therapy that tends towards the condition of silence and achieves its success, not in finding a solution to a problem, but in making the problem vanish. Wittgenstein also links written and spoken language with the visual: 'a picture held us captive. And we could not get outside it, for it lay in our language and language seemed to repeat it to us inexorably.'[67] That is precisely what Beckett does: he blends the unusual use of language, much of it using a code he has developed that he only shares with the most indefatigable of his readers, to put over a complete *wash* or atmosphere that attracts playgoers and readers to the works in question, without their quite knowing why, just as many are attracted by the atmosphere of works which could be in any of many disciplines, containing, for instance, an element of the occult, the supernatural or the ghostly. The invention of a code to which they feel they have privileged access is attractive to academics, which is why academe has embraced Beckett more than any other modern author. But many of them are so busy checking the code that they often miss the whole significance of the work itself.

Beckett's writing can be enjoyed on many levels: a deep understanding of sources and of his hidden thoughts and meanings is no more necessary than it is to know all of Wagner's *Leitmotifs* to enjoy the operas. Unfortunately the *wash* has attracted many producers who have not bothered to study the plays for their different levels of meaning, nor even to read the stage directions with any attention; these are usually attention-seeking directors who simply use the atmosphere created by the mix of interesting and unusual stage pictures, and the poetic power of the language, as a vehicle for some clever idea of their own that may have no connection or relevance to the work. That is when the audience becomes puzzled because such productions rob the plays of their essential dignity, conviction and universality, which enable the audience first to trust, then to penetrate and finally to feel the poetic truth of the play. Full understanding comes later, but only when it is the Beckett play, not a distortion, that is presented.

It is not even necessary for someone staging a Beckett play to comprehend its deeper meanings. The author has provided for that with the great detail and precision that he invested in the printed directions, respecting movement, gesture, timing and stage picture. Reliable treatises, based on Beckett's rehearsal notebooks, have now appeared that analyse the plays, including the stage directions, in such historical detail, and with the weight of Beckett's own authority behind them, that it is almost impossible to go wrong. Paradoxically, instead of limiting the producer to a single vision of the work, the authors *Notebooks* do the contrary and within the framework of text and stage direction there is great scope for interpretation and nuance. There are so many double and triple meanings and verbal climaxes that different productions can emphasis qu te different aspects of the same play. Beckett himself did this: the reason for the shift in emphasis often being differences between the actors themselves or the propensity of an audience to grasp one principal point rather than another.

The language of the plays contain a lyricism and a rhetoric that enables it to put over its own poetic truth. The language of movement that accompanies it tends to be more symbolic; the two work together to create the kind of attention that otherwise only music, especially opera in its higher reaches, can command. There is much in common between what Beckett does on stage and the way that opera works. Both use all the resources that the assembled stage elements can provide, both work primarily through sensation, then emotion, then reason. Beckett has always compared his work to music and it is by this route that many people can come to appreciate his work. Shakespeare's plays are similar in this respect, and Beckett is probably closer to Shakespeare than any other writer, even than Joyce whom he imitated in the very early work. Shakespeare and Beckett create a kind of opera through the harmonious and heightened use of words, where all the elements of opera, other than the music itself, are present. Timing is very important and Beckett gives great weight to pauses, rhythms and word stresses. That is the reason that it is possible to see a Beckett play many times, the pleasure growing with familiarity and each new insight. As with music, Beckett yields up his treasures little by little, and familiarity enhances the understanding and the appreciation.

The prose works and the poetry contain the same coded messages, but the stage picture has to be put by the author into the reader's mind without stage directions. Each of us has his own idea of what Molloy looks like (to me rather like Pozzo, but dressed like Estragon) and we visualise the settings for the novels, and see in our minds the places where they happen. The description of the countryside in the first pages of *Molloy*, where A and C (Abel and Cain) can be seen walking from a higher point was clear in my mind, and I instantly recognised the scene when I went to Roussillon, where Beckett hid during the war. The hill-top village commands the surrounding countryside in all directions; anyone on any road can be seen from a distance. The meaning of A and C becomes clear. The first is a friendly presence, the latter sinister, such as a German patrol on its way to the village, which would necessitate the departure of anyone not wanting to be questioned. There is, of course, no hint of this in the novel.

In such short texts as *Enough, Imagination Dead Imagine* or *The Lost Ones* the background is minutely described. These three non-dramatic works have all been given stage performances, where what we hear we would otherwise be reading. The pictures in our minds read or heard, become the same, although in the more celebrated concrete stage realisation of David Warrilow's *The Lost Ones*, where he moves tiny figures around inside a hollow upright cylinder, while delivering the text as a recitation, in spite of the brilliance that this particular actor has always brought to his Beckettian performances, something becomes lost, the possibility of each seeing it in his own way. Beckett always resisted the various attempts of actors and producers to portray his novels, especially *Molloy*, either on the stage or on film. The actor who would have embodied him perfectly was Patrick Magee, for whose voice Beckett had written *Krapp's Last Tape* and whose BBC recordings of the entire *Trilogy* are probably unsurpassable. But even Magee was never allowed to portray him and Beckett was right. Molloy remains one of Beckett's most powerful creations just because we are never quite sure what he looks like.

Association plays a large part in all of Beckett's work. In the plays each stage movement has its particular relevance, so that in *Waiting for Godot* the perambulations of the four characters around the stage, especially of the two principal ones, are meant to echo events referred to in the text. The most notable of these is the Crucifixion. When Vladimir reproaches Estragon for comparing himself and his suffering to Christ's, the latter answers, 'All my life I've compared myself to him', pointing out a minute later that Christ was better off in a warm, dry climate where 'they crucified quick'. There is Vladimir's reference to 'every man his little cross. (Sighs). Till he dies. (Afterthought). And is forgotten.'[68]

Beckett's rehearsal notebooks, which have been preserved at Reading University, contain the author's drawings of the *Godot* stage movements in the productions he directed: cruciform designs abound, both in the walks of the characters and the crossed heaps of bodies when Pozzo falls in the second act and is unable to rise. Besides crosses there are many circles to describe how the characters should move around the stage, and the origin of these is Dante's concentric circles of hell. So the visual language and the spoken combine to create a new dramatic vocabulary, in its way as stylised as Chinese opera, every gesture having significance. The audience should find its initial fascination with this new non-naturalistic, sometimes balletic and mimetic drama, gradually turning into curiosity and the desire to know more, as it begins to realise the symbolical quality of the play. There is already a specialised Beckett audience just as there is a specialised public for Shakespeare or Wagner. The plainness of the decor in *Waiting for Godot* only enhances the richness of the underlying plan, which is to convey to the audience the play's message that life is never-ending misery, which, all the same, can be entertaining to watch. Vladimir and Estragon are sustained nevertheless by hope, however much deferred, and by the sharing of that misery with others, which is the basis of good companionship. The play does not make that message about human misery to the audience directly: no one would come if it did. But it should and it can make the audience feel it, and be changed by it.

Two predictable reactions to a production of *Waiting for Godot* are, first that the audience noticeably cheers up by the time the play finishes, comparing its own lot to that far worse one endured by Beckett's characters (the darker plays of O'Neill and O'Casey produce a similar reaction), and secondly that it develops a sympathy and better understanding of those unfortunates one sees daily in the streets whose lives are similar to those of Vladimir and Estragon; a natural revulsion and fear is replaced by compassion. The third reaction is that of those who already know the play well, one of aesthetic enjoyment and a renewed philosophical contemplation of the human predicament.

The symbols of Christianity, the life of Christ and the medieval world of Dante's *Divine Comedy*, all play an integral part in *Waiting for Godot* and the same elements are found throughout Beckett's work. The fascination with Christ is mainly with the terrible death, which is supposed to have brought some benefit to mankind. If he died for us, what did we get out of that cruel execution, which was also the fate of so many thousands of others in the heyday of the Roman Empire? From what did our saviour save us? And for what? For two thousand years man has lived with the Christian myth, its purpose never satisfactorily explained, a well-worn chronicle, with no outside objective confirmation, of a Jewish heretic's life and death, which has served the same main purpose of all religions, which is to maintain respect for authority and obtain obedience through habit and fear.

All the scepticism of the renegade is present in *Waiting for Godot*. In other Beckett works of the same period the protest against religion is expressed in anger. Christianity, like its counterparts in the other major monotheistic religions, is not a philosophy, or a system of thought that admits new discovery, but an enclosed self-contained world of belief and dogma, that only occasionally, and with the greatest reluctance, allows its circumference to be stretched a little to admit new knowledge that cannot be suppressed, as in the years after Galileo's time and Darwin's. Christianity can be ignored, parodied or attacked, sometimes, and effectively, with too much love by those who would like to expose it without evoking a reaction from the church itself. Beckett's attack on Christianity, because much of his work is in essence just that, is largely effected through smothering it in this way. He loves it to death by wearing away at it through the non-devotional curiosity of his characters in *Waiting for Godot* (or the devotional questioning of Moran), picking at the absurdities, raising the questions the priests never raise, and letting it be seen with the clothes gradually removed. Here, because they cannot read the code, the religious bodies do not see what is happening. Devotional religion is a language of its own, depending on the cadence and the imagery of the scriptures, imposed from childhood, appealing to human insecurity and fear, and the willingness of the adherents to accept any answer rather than none, and with the imprimatur of authority gratefully accepted. It is self-contained, feeding on itself, anxious to keep out any whiff of negation from the outside world. The language of philosophy, at least in modern times, and to some extent going back to the Enlightenment, has been an attempt to offer an alternative to religion for a thinking minority in a society that has achieved a reasonable balance of tolerance, which, while unstable and volatile, allows coexistence and the spread of knowledge, inevitable in an age of instant communication. Technology has made censorship empirically impossible, and only self-censorship, imposed on the individual by himself in obedience to authority from outside, by coreligionists, can keep dogma alive. The rise of fundamentalism, usually supported by blind nationalism, also makes this possible.

In the early middle ages there was a period referred to by Friedrich Heer[69] as the World of the Three Rings, Christian, Jewish (which more or less included the non-Christian Greek) and Muslim, that for a short time achieved peaceful coexistence and mutual respect and tolerance. The worlds did not touch or overlap, each being self-contained, and they could therefore not harm each other. The only worry of each was heresy within its own ranks. But circles so close must in time come into contact and infiltrate each other. It was the imperialist desire for land, power and to proselytise, led by the Western Church and the fanaticism of St. Bernard, that broke down the peace of the old world, leading to the Crusades and the Muslim counter-offensive. We would appear at the end of the twentieth century to be entering a similar era. Religions and nationalistic fundamentalisms are on the increase. Both depend on a fashion of irrationalism for their success. The tolerance that developed during the Enlightenment, that has grown through the last two centuries, is breaking down, and that irrationalism is not only present but spreading like a virus, primarily in the third world, but also in the democracies where the electorate is much of the time persuaded to vote against its own best interests by the tactics and chicaneries of the public relations industries employed by political parties, whose armoury of psychological and technological weaponry is tremendous.

The significance of Beckett's work in such an age is doubly important, because it flies in the face of society's newly found dependence on short-term solutions and on the values that lie behind it, which are a formula for catastrophe. Beckett is, in the very best sense, profoundly subversive. He was lucky to have lived in his own time, deadly as it was, probing a murky world growing murkier, with his sharp intelligence; lucky because he could never quite hide his propensity for martyrdom. He did not have to become a Bruno, which in another time would probably have been his fate. He was torn, as all heretics and renegades are torn, by the culture they have to leave behind, because it is intolerable and unbelievable, in order to build an alternative structure that can never be fully satisfactory, because it offers no emotional relief and will always incur the opposition of the majority. But if one can achieve freedom in one's own mind, one is lucky, and Beckett was lucky in his time. Could it be that Lucky in *Waiting for Godot* derives his name from his having acquired the ability to think as Beckett thought, to have the will to face the consequences of that thought and the grim satisfaction of seeing Man 'waste and pine' beneath his eyes, with the created world of vegetation and animal life reverting to a cold abode of stones? Lucky is free in his mind: that, for a philosopher, is luck enough.

All his life Beckett struggled with language, dissatisfied with its inability to express exactly the meaning that always just eluded him. What he nearly achieved was a scream of agony containing the total impotence of a human life. If unbearable enough it might have satisfied him. But that is not what concerns his readers. His writing was a miracle of expression: no one ever came nearer to turning language into music. English best suited his poetry, but his best poems, or at least the most beautiful of them, were mainly those he wrote in French. Those he translated back had a flow and a cadence that perfectly conveyed the passing thought. Beckett's poems concisely state some of his most important insights: they were almost condensations of the philosophy that went into whole novels. But unlike the fiction, especially the *Trilogy* and the later shorter works, the poems are very personal and about his own eyes seeing the world, not looking at our 'muckheap' through the vision of those whom society rejects, his hobo heroes. The amount of self-revelation and meaning that he packs into the following poem is typical, but there are significant differences between the French original and the English version that follows it, showing how language both limits and extends meaning.

> je suis ce cours de sable qui glisse
> entre le galet et la dune
> la pluie d'été pleut sur ma vie
> sur moi ma vie qui me fuit me poursuit
> et finira le jour de son commencement
>
> cher instant je te vois
> dans ce rideau de brume qui recule
> où je n'aurai plus à fouler ces long seuils mouvants
> et vivrai le temps d'une porte
> qui s'ouvre et se referme
>
> my way is in the sand flowing
> between the shingle and the dune
> the summer rain rains on my life
> on me my life harrying fleeing
> to it beginning to its end
>
> my peace is there in the receding mist
> when I cease from treading these long shifting thresholds
> and live the space of a door
> that opens and shuts'[70]

The double meaning in the French first line of *suis* implies that he both identifies himself as a part of the sand, like the handful of dust that we shall all become, and that his path through it is circular leading to his ending. The double meaning is lost in the English, where he also no longer addresses the *cher instant* but glimpses instead the peace he is seeking, the peace of oblivion. It is also interesting to note in the English last line of the first stanza that he is going *to*, not *from* his birth, in other words back to where he came from, a concept that had impressed him in Schopenhauer, whose opinion was that in death we return to what we were before our conception.

Beckett's fear that we may return in another life or go to some intermediate resting place surfaces many times. In *Embers*, the radio play, he pictures a form of hell, consisting of 'small chat to the babbling of Lethe about the good old days when we wished we were dead'.[71] The good old days are what the tramps in *Waiting for Godot* are living through until they join 'the dead voices'. They are what the thinking dead go over endlessly in their minds, like the threesome in *Play*, rerunning their past lives over and over.

Beckett's equation of birth and death does not quite take into account the months of life inside the mother's womb, but he frequently refers to it as the one possibly endurable time of his life.

> ... but I give her credit, though she is my mother, for what she tried to do for me. And I forgive her for having jostled me a little in the first months and spoiled the only endurable, just endurable period of my enormous history.[72]

Beckett was much interested in a lecture that he attended in 1935, given by Carl Jung. The psychiatrist spoke of a young girl who had never been properly born and the thought worried Beckett for years. Jung does not appear to have explained what he meant by 'never been properly born', but he must have meant either that the trauma of birth had somehow been bypassed, leaving a gap in the emotional history of the patient—Beckett almost certainly connected the state of mind of Lucia Joyce, whose unrequited love for himself as a young Irishman in Paris, was blamed, at least by himself, for a life-long mental illness, with Jung's patient—or that the person concerned did not really exist in terms of having a full consciousness. The incident is related in *All That Fall* by Mrs. Rooney, who tells us that the girl eventually died. There is obviously an identification with Mrs. Rooney's own daughter, who never grew up, and the radio play ends with the news that the reason for the train being late is that another little girl had fallen under the wheels. Throughout *All That Fall* the tune of *Death and the Maiden*, the dirge-like Schubert song, appears as a *Leitmotif*, the virgin carried away by Death before she has known love. The appeal of the song to Beckett was as much in the words as in the music, because Death says he will be a considerate lover and that the maiden will sleep well in his arms. The theme of death as a happy haven comes up again in *Krapp's Last Tape* and again in *Footfalls* where the spectral daughter, whom one sees pacing the stage is, like Mrs. Rooney's Minnie, dead, probably prenatally, because that is another way of not being born. A whole Beckett code has been constructed around the theme of birth, prenatal existence, mother-love, and death, where the same thoughts and references recur and add new aspects to the pattern. It is a code that has to be learned little by little as interest in and knowledge of Beckett's work grows from the haunting verbal music and atmosphere that the plays create and the cadences that are woven through the novels and poems. Study of Beckett is as rewarding, and in a very similar way, to studying Beethoven. A little research is immensely rewarding, a lot even more so.

Music and its associations are a part of the code that lies behind much of Beckett's use and invention of language. Where there is a text attached to music, as in a song, the words of the text become part, sometimes the most important part, of the association. This is true in particular of the Schubert songs, 'Death and the Maiden' and 'Nacht und Träume', the latter giving its title to a late television play where the picture seen by the viewer echoes the words of the song which are heard with the music. Beckett takes his associations from many sources; other notable musical examples are the 'Merry Widow Waltz' in *Happy Days* and the Irish version of the hymn 'Now the Day is Over' in *Krapp's Last Tape*, each giving a deeper meaning to the situations of the protagonists, an epiphany illuminating the present moment as future time, with all its sinister implications, moves into the present.

Mention of Beethoven is not accidental. The two artists had many similarities, especially in the romantic strain implicit in their work. The *Sturm und Drang* era was an important influence on all of Beckett's work, more obvious in the early writings, but still much present in the middle and late. The work of both Beethoven and Beckett can be divided into three quite distinct periods, the first a continuation and extension of an existing tradition (Mozart and Joyce respectively), the second a full flowering of a new order of artistic creation, destined to become the trademark of the artist (the symphonies from the *Eroica* onward, the Rasumovsky Quartets and works contemporary with them in the case of Beethoven; *Waiting for Godot*, *Endgame*, and the *Trilogy*, in the case of Beckett), the last period for both is a move into philosophical introspection and resignation to death. In Beckett's case, the late period is one of a tightly controlled compression, a minimum number of words carrying a maximum weight of thought; with it there is an interlinked system of codified references to familiar underlying preoccupations, but they are often differently stated with new allusions and metaphorical images coming into the work.

How It Is is the watershed into the late period in the same way that the *Hammerklavier* sonata of 1821 presages Beethoven's move to a new form and outlook, while still identifiable as a middle period work. Started in French in 1959, *Comment c'est* was published in Paris two years later and the author's translation into English in 1964. The extreme originality of the text, conceived as a monologue delivered in gulps of breath as the narrator swims through a sea of mud, gasping for air, was such that I organised, before publication, a Sunday afternoon reading of parts of the text, together with other more familiar and accessible Beckett extracts, in the same *Criterion Theatre* that had once played host to the original English production of *Waiting for Godot* when it transferred from the tiny *Arts Theatre Club*. Beckett came to London to rehearse the actors, but did not attend the readings by Jack Macgowran and Patrick Magee, which were followed by public discussion, chaired by Martin Esslin. The event was well attended by the public and the literary press, and I made a recording of one long passage from *How It Is*, that, sent to reviewers with the book, helped considerably in obtaining intelligent coverage for this important publication, that otherwise might easily have been ignored or dismissed. Beckett's reputation, although not then at its height, was well-enough established, especially among those who had been students when *Waiting for Godot* became the talking point of intellectual Britain, for a work of such difficulty—it was also his last full-length novel—to be successful.

How It Is is verbal panic, filtered through the mind by the rhythms of the swimmer, trying to stay afloat as long as possible in spite of the downward tug, his current thought interspersed with past memories, especially of the author's boyhood, and of 'an ancient voice . . . the voice of us all as many as we are . . . [referring to] days of great gaiety thicker than on earth since the age of gold above in the light the leaves fallen dead.'[73] The lack of punctuation, the reader having to judge for himself where and how to separate phrases, each representing a gulp for air, with the frequent paragraphs, about six to a page of varying lengths, each representing a moment when the body allows itself to relax briefly before resuming the struggle, makes *How It Is* a difficult book to read, but once one has grasped the principles of its construction and begun to savour the extraordinary power of the language, and the protagonist's will to survive that it conveys, it becomes a joy.

Beckett's long late period then properly begins. A series of short texts followed *How It Is*: *Imagination Dead Imagine* (1965), *Enough* and *Ping* (1966) *Lessness* (1969), *The Lost Ones* (1971), *For to End Yet Again* (1976).[74] These combine glimpses of humanity, or of human remnants in situations akin to Dante's hell, all metaphors of a kind, all painful, some not unlike newspaper reports of the scene of a massacre or battlefield. *Imagination Dead Imagine* has already been described in Chapter 2. *Enough* is about a master-pupil relationship characterised by absolute trust together with total subservience on the part of the pupil, a relationship of ageing affection with some sexual references, but of the past described in the present. It is written in the style of the *Trilogy* and could almost describe a marriage where the younger passive pupil follows the

master in everything; the reference to 'old breasts' suggests
that the pupil is a woman.

Lessness is the telling in six voices, each speaking only a
sentence at a time, of a disaster that overtook a tribe. The
voices are not identified, following each other in the order that
Beckett selected, but he did separate them for a BBC broadcast
with six readers. In twenty-four paragraphs the voices are per-
mutated, each one with his own few sentences, repeated in a
different order. The terrible past event could be a nuclear disaster, a natural cataclysm, a massacre, a war, although the
references to deformities suggest the first. The picture of devastation is shattering and enables Beckett, as ever, to distil
lines of poetic beauty and remoteness, like the remoteness of
God viewing events on earth, as in the last line: 'Figment
dawn dispeller of figments and the other called dusk.'

The Lost Ones is a parable of human life. Little figures
inhabit the interior of an upright cylinder, the top covered and
so far unreachable. There are many theories about what might
lie outside the cylinder and if it might be possible to escape
to an outside world, either by burrowing through the walls or
by making a hole in the top. The people also dig into the walls
to make niches to inhabit and tunnels to connect them, or to
explore for whatever might be found. They run up and down
ladders endlessly to get to the niches and tunnels. There is a
great shortage of ladders, so that the inhabitants have to
queue to use them. Some of the bodies are in constant motion,
others occasionally pause, others sit listlessly against the
walls, stirring occasionally into activity, while others still, the
weaker members, try to get a corner to sit in more comfortably, but are constantly ousted by the stronger. All the activity
is, like life, pointless, but there is nevertheless great curiosity
about the world outside the cylinder and many faiths are built
on the different theories. Unlike the other short texts of this
period, *The Lost Ones* is about life itself, not some future hell
or state of devastation. But it is no more cheerful for that.

There is a change of tone in the works that followed in the
mid Seventies. *Still* appeared in 1975, a contemplative picture
of a man reflecting, listening, quite still, at an open window

at the end of a dark day when 'the sun shines out at last and
goes down.' Its quietism is something new and it was added
to the *Fizzles* (USA title), six short texts translated from French,
which came out in the UK as *For to End Yet Again* in 1976, the
year also of French publication. These have a similarity,
though not in tone, to the *Texts for Nothing*, which are contemporary with *Waiting for Godot*. Both series of texts are outbursts at or about the human tragedy, but the later series are
significantly more muted and accepting; the mood is one of
sadness rather than anger:

> . . . simply stay still, standing before a window, one hand on the
> wall, the other clutching your shirt, and see the sky, a long gaze,
> but no, gasps and spasms, a childhood sea, other skies, another
> body.[75]

This is not Molloy speaking, either from his mother's bed
or from the ditch into which he has fallen after being lost in
the woods. It is not a wild romantic Neitzschean figure, cursing God for the evil he wreaks or permits. It is the ageing,
comfortably-off, intellectual pessimist, who has a window to
look out of, a clean shirt to wear and who, when he stops
standing, will have a chair to sit on. It is Beckett himself, the
wartime traumas long past, the years of struggle to write, to
get published, to earn a decent living, all behind him, now
able to forget himself and look at the world from a distance
with greater understanding and with a deep, unbearable sadness at the waste of human effort, the continuing cruelty, the
inability of mankind to do anything to make its lot better,
reduce suffering and to strive for a more civilised existence.
The curse of Adam is still there, and he knows it always will
be. Now, Beckett, with no need to write more, knowing he
can do nothing to change conditions except by helping a few
individuals, goes on writing because it passes the time. Along
with the texts there are the plays: *Not I* (1973), *That Time*
(1976), *Footfalls* and *Ghost Trio* (1976) '. . .but the clouds. . .'
(1977), *Piece of Monologue* (1979) which is really another *Fizzle*.
The plays of the same period are nearer to the earlier work,
the protagonists all dying or near death, seen as they

approach it, accepting, but cursing both life and its end. But they all accept it. In his prose texts it is the author who is talking; in the plays the dramatic imagination is still at work, finding new visual or metaphorical ways of presenting human tragedy to audiences, creating new characters, the stage atmosphere becoming ever more ghostly and unreal. In the works of the Eighties, which include six short plays, a number of prose fragments and shorter texts, of which the last, *Stirrings Still*, is a moving picture of an old writer, unable to go out, but who does go out in his imagination, Beckett is waiting for his own end to come with mingled acceptance and disquiet. 'One wonders about the future,' he said to me in his last months, and he had a little earlier sent me the following:

> go end there
> one fine day
> where never till now
> till as much to say
> no matter where
> no matter when.[76]

It is the stoicism of Hamm at the end. Beckett's language in the final prose and poems became simpler and direct. The spirit of stoicism had entered into the language itself.

But before the last works he had written three extraordinary novellas: *Company* first appeared in 1980, *Ill Seen Ill Said* in 1981 in France, and a year later in Britain, and *Worstward Ho* in 1983. They were republished as a trilogy in 1989 under the title *Nohow On*. The first is a solipsistic narrative of a man, alone in the dark, listening to voices, which at the end, it is admitted, are all his own. The voices are his company and so are the anecdotes, mainly from childhood and young adulthood, that enliven the text as memories, and give us wonderful glimpses into the way the author remembered his own early years. The last, *Worstward Ho*, is a brief, very stylised and compressed history of the creation of man and his ultimate destiny to go out to conquer space. The style, constantly juxtaposing everything that belongs to pure imagination, whether possible or not, with its opposite, becomes a new language. It is based on the same process, the chemical mixtures and the molecular broth that created life and all existence, in which the universe we know probably began. The second novella will be discussed in the next chapter. Here in the context of language and philosophy, *Worstward Ho* pictures the endless activity of nature to *create* against all possible odds, bringing one element into contact with another until at last two or more fuse and the impossible becomes possible, the uncreateable is created, and then it looks for another fusion. No scientist could better describe the act of creation. Creation derived from nothing is doomed to fail, but if it can fail better it may ultimately fail less, and eventually not fail at all. The impossible happens. What a tragedy, because the most horrible thing that can happen is, of course, success! But nature will always, in the end, win somehow, by creating something. So evil triumphs once again as all the mixtures and rubbings move towards some accidental but concrete created end.

> First the body. No. First the place. No. First both. Now either. Now the other. Sick of the either try the other. Sick of it back sick of the either. So on. Somehow on. Till sick of both. Throw up and go. Where neither. Till sick of there. Throw up and back. The body again. Where none. The place again. Where none. Try again. Fail again. Better again. Or better worse. Fail worse again. Still worse again. Till sick for good. Throw up for good. Go for good. Where neither for good. Good and all.[77]

In the next paragraph, the impossible happens:

> It stands. What? Yes. Say it stands. Had to up in the end and stand.

Beckett has become Prospero. He has found a way to make magic with words and at the same time to give us an insight into the messy method of God's or nature's creation and evince a Schopenhauerean horror at the implications.

In an early essay (1929)[78] opening a volume of tributes to Joyce's *Work in Progress*, which was to become *Finnegans Wake*, the young Beckett had started to explore literary and philosophical aesthetics as a writer. The essay, written under the direct instructions of his idol and guru, had as its purpose to connect Joyce to Dante and to bring in two intermediate influences whom Joyce told Beckett had contributed to his thought, namely Giordano Bruno (1548–1600), a Dominican monk who was burnt at the stake for heresy, and Giambattista Vico (1668–1774) who absorbed and regurgitated some of Bruno's ideas, but, as Beckett points out, was careful not to name his source. In his essay Beckett investigates social and historical philosophy in a way he was never to do again. Bruno was basically a pantheist, believing that God and nature are one, giving monadism its modern meaning, whereby we come from and return to God at death, all material and spiritual substance being one and indivisible. Vico, a social and historical thinker as well as a theologian, analysed the growth and decline of civilisations in a manner not unlike that of Karl Marx two centuries later, seeing every society pass through three stages, the divine, the heroic and the human, and he describes the growth of law as developed out of the need to control man's baser instincts.

> Legislation considers man as he is, in order to create of him good practices in human society; as, from violence, avarice and ambition, which are the three vices prevalent throughout the whole of mankind, it creates the army, the commerce and the court, and thus the strength, wealth and wisdom of states; and from these three great vices, which would certainly destroy the human species on earth, it creates civil happiness.[79]

Beckett's study of Vico for the *Exagmination* essay concentrates, not on the optimistic side of Vico's analysis, but on the decadence and decline that must be present in all progress. Vico recognised that civilisation is circular (another link to Dante), but what Beckett carries forward is the concept that the corruptions of one era, those of Scipio and Caesar for example, are the energies of the next, those of Caesar and Tiberius. Beckett's conviction that man is unimprovable may well have had its intellectual beginning in his brooding on Vico. He accepts Vico's six stages of human motivation, necessity, utility, convenience, pleasure, luxury, abuse of luxury, leading over the centuries to a high, then a corrupt civilisation, which will eventually collapse into barbarism as the Roman Empire did, but although he never says so directly—the purpose of the essay was more to please Joyce than to air his own preoccupations—it is clear that he saw little point in building a system for the advancement of human well-being if it was only to collapse in the end, and the inevitable 'interdestruction', after centuries of misery, once again come round to the point where 'the Phoenix of Society arises out of their ashes'.

Beckett defines Vico's poetics as a form of literary monadism, a unity where form and content cannot be separated and poetry and language are not dualistic, developing simultaneously, like society. He then transfers this concept to Joyce's work, pointing out, in one of his most quoted phrases, that 'His [Joyce's] great work is not *about* something; *it is that something itself*.[80] That statement was eventually to be even more applicable to his own work, especially the later texts, and above all to *Worstward Ho*, where the form of the language, and the view of man and nature and the whole of the existence we inhabit, are all indivisibly part of the same philosophical concept, a universe endlessly creating more creation by the chance meeting and fusion of its elements, with no awareness or concern for consequence. Put differently, it is a concept of a blind, creation-hungry God, heedless and unstoppable, creating into eternity.

7

Looking at God

Samuel Beckett lost his faith early, probably at about sixteen, but the mythology of Christianity remained with him all his life, and he was always interested, in a general sense, in comparative religion and metaphysics. Those who have described him as 'God haunted' were right, but the haunting had a mystical quality to it, not a devotional one. There is also an element of fear in his relationship to what he could not believe, but which seemed to be lurking always in the background of his mind, like a small animal's fascination towards its predator. When Estragon says that all his life he has compared himself to Christ, it is Beckett talking: his own loss of faith had never quelled his interest in the story of Christ and his painful, lingering death on the cross. His self-identification was always with the victim. In one short evocative prose fragment,[81] found after his death in the Beckett collection at Austin, Texas, there is a thinly disguised account of the *via dolorosa*, depicting Christ with his cross on the way to execution: the author's empathy with the subject is clear. The Christian references in *Waiting for Godot* are numerous because the tramps pass part of the time with biblical speculations, and, for example, the story of the two thieves, one saved by Christ and the other delivered up to hellfire, is both a comment on one of the gospels and a reflection on divine justice. Beckett, however, as an adult, never identifies the suffering Christ with God. Christ is man. As a 'saviour' he is only an object of sarcastic derision. Beckett's interest in God is of a quite different order.

Waiting for Godot is about man's sufferings during his lifetime and his helplessness in the face of a world that can never be understood, where the way is not beautiful, nor the wayfarers good. Beckett has stated, quite definitely, that Godot is not God, which of course in any real sense he is not, but in his apparent remoteness he is very like the God that the two tramps need, a 'saviour' to help them out of their dilemma, but one who never comes. Godot is described as an old man with a white beard, and it is clear that when Vladimir hears this from the boy at the end of the play and interjects 'Christ have mercy upon us!' the thought of God has gone through his head. God is usually pictured by Beckett's characters as conventionally as he is presented to children in Sunday School, and by priests to the unquestioning believer with no desire to think about religion, who wants only to be told what to believe and what to expect after death. The various voices that speak to Beckett's characters are all in their heads, but what is important is what and where they think they are, and what the source of the voices would be if they were not just invented or imagined. Many Beckett characters are, like Joan of Arc, totally guided by their voices. The *Texts for Nothing*, thirteen extraordinary monologues, are all voices: some appear to be dead, even buried, all are cursing and railing at the source of all their misery, their rhetorical richness enabling much and many meanings to be read into them. They belong to the fecund two-year period when the author had put himself under siege and locked himself away to pour out as much as possible of what he wanted to write before the growth in his cheek, which he thought signalled his end, took its effect, to produce *Waiting for Godot* and the *Trilogy*. God was much thought about and much mocked in the early work, or rather man looking for God was mocked, because it is a waste of time to mock God. But in the masterpieces of the middle period, to which I am coming next, the ways of looking at and thinking about God are many, and they underlie the tone, the style and the philosophy of the work.

Much of what follows in this chapter is speculative, much is not. It should be said, once again, that it is no more necessary for the general reader to investigate the sources of the middle period works than it is necessary to know what was going on in Beethoven's mind when he was writing the Rasumovsky Quartets, or even the symphonies, to appreciate them fully. But the very nature of Beckett's work invites investigation, which is one of the reasons that he never liked to discuss it, and why he hid away so carefully so many of his sources in metaphor and parable.

In my own conversations with Beckett, which went on from the middle Fifties until his death in 1989, we discussed his work very little, except in so far as it was necessary professionally to go over those details, mainly technical that concern a publisher-editor and his author. We would talk about the things that interested us while walking in the country, in London or in Paris, sometimes during the day, but more often at night while eating or roaming around the streets of Montparnasse where he lived, sometimes playing chess, or billiards, or even ping-pong, and then ending the night, very late, with a beer. When he was with academics, their prepared questions at the ready, usually slipping them in when Beckett had dropped his guard a little, he was often milked for information, and when in the mood he would sometimes answer written questions by correspondence. But he did not enjoy the attention of academics, especially when they were incapable of relaxed general conversation. Out of circumspection, it was only very occasionally that I would ask Beckett to resolve a puzzle for me, and that mostly in the last years. Sometimes when I told him of a guess or a discovery that we both knew was true, he would be surprised, usually not particularly pleased at having a secret meaning uncovered, and occasionally he would avoid answering directly, saying sometimes that he could not remember. But at bottom, Beckett appreciated the interest shown in his work, if sincere, although he much preferred to be read without too much probing into what lay under the language and the situations portrayed.

My relationship with Beckett was one of collegial friendship, that of master-pupil in a sense, because I was twenty-one years younger, and I did not want to jeopardise that relationship. I always learned a great deal when talking about literature, world affairs and those intellectual and aesthetic interests we shared, like music and painting, and tastes such as food and wine. Many little crumbs came my way from his mind, but I never made notes, either at the time or later, as an academic would have done, and some of our deeper conversations, about philosophy, science (of which I knew little), the ideas of Bergson or the epics of Dante for instance, went on all night, with Beckett often quoting long passages from memory. I usually remembered little the next morning, aware of having spent an exhilarating night and suffering from a hangover. Beckett, until he became moderately abstemious in his last twenty years, had a much better head for drink than I, so while I cannot claim to remember much detail from our discussions—and we were not always alone, but sometimes with a group or with friends met accidentally at the Coupole or the Falstaff late at night—I do remember the general tenor of his attitudes, the depth of his reading and knowledge, and many of the sources of his opinions, what I would call, in brief, the *wash* of his mind.

Molloy is one of the world's great novels, and it will probably always be as central to his prose writing as *Waiting for Godot* is to his drama. It can be seen either as a novel on its own or as the first part of the *Trilogy*, but he did not object to individual publication, provided it was by the same publisher. The novels of the *Trilogy* are connected by several internal references; all of Beckett's early characters seem to be encompassed in the minds of the later ones, and there is a similarity and development of style between the three novels of the *Trilogy*; but there is no real reason why they cannot be read as individual works: one does not follow from another, and they are no more connected than are the other fictions. All of Beckett's work has a unity that makes it whole and complete, interconnected and interreferential, but it still consists of separate and self-sufficient units. My analysis of the religious content is partly speculative, although some of it has been deduced by others before me, and there is a little that has been admitted by Beckett himself.

The *Trilogy*, especially the first part of it, is the most puzzling, ambiguous and difficult to analyse of any of the work. But *Molloy*, in spite of that, is perfectly straightforward to read, a story of two quests and their endings, with a missing link in the circular first narrative, which starts with Molloy beginning to record what has happened to him, not sure how he got to where he is from the place where the narrative ends. It is full of allusions, of parable within parable, puzzling names and parallel situations, as well as parallel people. We have to assume that much of it comes from Beckett's own experiences, especially during the war. Biblical references abound from both the Old and the New Testaments, and like Joyce he uses and refers to characters and incidents out of the *Odyssey*. Not every reference can be followed very far: some are obviously there because the author obviously noticed at the time 'a neatness of identification, between an association and what he was writing' and there is no more to it than that. The impact of his experiences working in the Resistance, and on the run from the Gestapo, is difficult to pinpoint in the *Trilogy*, much more so than in *Waiting for Godot*, but Molloy's descriptions of his manoeuvres to escape capture, of being a hunted animal, and Beckett's own indirect knowledge of what happened to his friends who underwent torture to extract information are all obviously relevant.

The division of *Molloy* into two parts and two quests is yet another Beckettian dualism that moves towards a unity. It is quite possible, given the parallel existences of the two protagonists, Molloy and Moran, that they are the same person, a dual personality, and that when Moran searches for Molloy he is searching for himself. John Pilling and John Fletcher, two of the more perspicacious critics who have written about Beckett's work, were each given some time by the author to ask questions, and, as they were serious and intelligent academics with outgoing personalities, he gave them rather more information than was normally his wont, which at least knocked out a number of false leads, though he would not go into the deeper meanings. However, he did tell Fletcher the order of the works written during Beckett's self-imposed 'siege' in the late Forties. It is important to know this because of the interreferential nature of the works: the sequence is *Molloy*, *Éleutheria* (a play published in 1995 and unperformed at time of writing this book), *Malone Dies*, *Waiting for Godot*, *The Unnamable*, the *Texts for Nothing*.[82] The order is not at all what might have been guessed: much in *Waiting for Godot* seems to open the way for *Malone*, and the *Texts for Nothing* would seem to be experiments to get the style that would find its apotheosis in *The Unnamable*. But what mostly concerns me here is the use of names and symbols that have a religious significance, or rather that throw some light on Beckett's attitude at the time to God.

Beckett's characters have names that all, or nearly all, have a special significance for the author. Molloy is an Irish name, but it is very close to Molly, a form of Mary, whose significance to Christians is considerable, and connotes a certain ideal of womanhood, non-sexual, innocent and pure. Mary, as the Blessed Virgin Mary, will come up again, later in this chapter. Nevertheless it is difficult to imagine a less feminine image than that of Beckett's Molloy, a prototypal outcast, with the grim sense of irony that we find in many tramps if we allow ourselves to talk to them. Whatever the connection in the author's mind, we can rule out that one is a metaphor for the other. The novel gives an accurate and very full portrait of a common character who in the past has been little examined by writers, although Dickens and some nineteenth-century French novelists have written of similar personalities, usually seen as criminals. It is conceivable that there is some connection between Molloy and Mary; he could be her son, in which case his torments might be those of Jesus and it is not hard to find similarities, but then the cross comes up so often in Beckett's work of this and later periods that not too much must be read into such references; there are many suffering wayfarers, and parallels between the wanderings of Jesus, of Molloy and other Beckett characters must be looked at in general terms. Moran's first name is Jacques, not far from Jesus, and so is his son's. J is not a very common letter in Beckett's work and Joseph, the father of Jesus is another J. Beckett certainly intended a connection, but he left no clues other than the work itself.

John Fletcher points out that Thom's Dublin directory[83] lists nearly all the proper names given, not only in the *Trilogy*, but in the earlier novels as well, which makes it even more difficult to probe them for referential clues. And Fletcher, consulting French directories, finds the same principle applies to the French names that Beckett has given to other characters. But Beckett's ingenuity at combining names and thoughts is impressive. Nothing can be taken for granted, but very little can be ruled out either.

Molloy is on a quest, for which many parallels can be found in literature, one of the closest being *The Pilgrim's Progress*. He is also the object of a quest. Moran, the private detective who is sent, in the second part of the novel, to find Molloy by his superior, Gaber, is a buttoned-up, pedantic, devout Catholic, whose attitudes nonetheless seem to belong more to the Irish Protestantism of Beckett's own early environment. Who is Gaber? He is sent by Youdi to bring a message to Moran. What springs to mind is the Annunciation, the New Testament episode where the Archangel Gabriel appears to the Virgin Mary to tell her that he will bring forth a child. Is Gaber Gabriel and Moran Mary? Obviously any parallel intended by the author cannot be that close because by no stretch of the imagination can one identify Mary with Moran, any more than with Molloy. But Youdi is very close to Yahweh (Jehovah), the Hebrew name for God that does not quite name him, but refers to him indirectly as The Lord. Yahweh emerges later in *The Unnamable*. It is reasonable to assume that Youdi is a metaphor for God. There are far too many theological references throughout the novel for a reader to be unaware of them, and it is never clear when the allusions are making a point and when Beckett is playing games to confuse his readers. But they add considerable spice and provoke thought. One should also not forget that Moses and Mohommed also have names beginning with M.

Beckett opens his essay on Joyce in *Our Exagmination* with an apt warning which applies equally well to attempts to analyse his own work: 'The danger lies in the neatness of identifications.' There is no neatness where the *Trilogy* is concerned: it is an intermingling of stories that resemble each other, but never exactly, of characters of which the same is true, and of references to names and events that owe their provenance principally to the Bible and to Dante's *Inferno*. The characters seem to metamorphose into each other; Malone even suggests that he was not always called that, as he struggles to sort out his own identity and history:

> ... it is too late now, or still too soon, I forget which, except that they have brought me the solution and conclusion of the whole sorry business, I mean the business of Malone (since that is what I am called now) and of the other, for the rest is no business of mine.[84]

In *The Unnamable* the confusion of the characters is even more prevalent, all of them, from the early prewar novels to the *Trilogy*, passing in procession before the narrator as if in a kind of Hell, and all present in his psyche and memory.

Beckett lays trails of allusion which lead the reader to suppositions that become absurd. The references to Youdi are perfectly consistent with his being God, but it is difficult to associate Molloy with anything other than suffering humanity; he is the total outsider, yet existing nevertheless under some kind of divine protection. There may be similarities between his journey and that of Bunyan's Christian, but Molloy is certainly not the Christ who was born to save humanity, a quest as dramatic in its failure as any in Beckett. Molloy is aware of Abel and Cain, although he only names them by their initials. They are remembered from his bed in their observed approaches to each other on a country road. The confrontation comes up at the beginning and the end of the book, but it is only at the end of his narrative, lying in a ditch, that Molloy remembers that one of them, obviously Cain, was carrying a club. Moran might well be Cain; he apparently kills a man he meets in the wilderness, who interrupts him when he is lighting a camp fire, although the action of killing is somehow erased from his mind a moment later; it does not occur to him that the victim might be the man he is seeking, Molloy!

The similarities between what is seen from a distance and what then happens in a different narrative are always striking. Abel and Cain are seen by Molloy to meet, but they separate without incident. They are seen from a height; both the flat countryside and the hilltop from which they are seen suggests

Roussillon. Saint Thomas Aquinas gives us a similar picture, which may have a bearing: 'the man who sees the whole road from a height sees simultaneously all those who are going along the road'. What Molloy sees in his mind's eye, in memory in bed, and perhaps once saw in reality, might well be not just Abel and Cain, but any of the characters from the Beckett world in the novel, repeating the biblical story. Who is the man Moran meets, who looks rather like himself (his brother? Baudelaire's *'mon semblable, mon frère'* for example?), who offers friendly advances, which are repulsed, and then is 'stretched on the ground, his head in a pulp'? If the deed is Moran's, is he then not Cain? Do Molloy and Moran ever really meet or do they always just miss each other? The unexplained loose ends in *Molloy* only end up in a series of puzzles, very like those in life, which the conventional novel, having to explain to the reader's satisfaction everything that happens and the reasons for it, cannot allow. Much of the fascination of *Molloy* is that so much is unexplained, which is also the principal characteristic that links this important work to the *nouveau roman*.

Seeking and finding belong to different worlds, and Beckett was preoccupied with the first, which we can identify with speculative philosophy, whereas finding has more to do with man's practical and scientific activities, each finding leading on to a further search. Philosophy never achieves complete answers, but is always getting a little closer to them, which is also Beckett's definition of his own creative quest, moving the rock-cliff a fraction further on. But doing so he becomes very like God, the creator creating into eternity, whereas contemplating philosophically, he can find reasons to object to that creation with all its consequences. There is always a paradox at the centre of Beckett's thinking, which emerges most strongly in the fiction, and nowhere more so than in *Molloy*, where Cain and Abel are moving through the same landscapes as Molloy and Moran, where no quest is completed, although perhaps, unknowingly, Moran, a total incompetent as a detective, does find Molloy, and Cain does find and kill Abel, and where Youdi's orders, which are never carried out, still require a report (which is Moran's narrative). Nearly all the characters who are not killed (Molloy kills, or very nearly does, the charcoal-burner, while Moran kills his look-alike) end as decrepit and ruined. The two narratives of *Molloy* are circular, intertwined, and contain as many non sequiturs as allusions, but the narrative meaning, in spite of all the puzzles, is very clear, and easily described. Two protagonists, of very different temperaments, cross each others' paths, but never knowingly meet. As in Beckett's mime *Act Without Words 2*, where one ambitious character with a work ethic (much like Moran) shares a suit with his energyless, sloppy, uncaring opposite (much like Molloy, although the analogy is less close), both come to roughly the same end, and in the case of the novel to the acceptance of failure. Moran's theological questionings to pass the time on his homeward journey are amusing and occasionally very subversive, as for instance, buried in the pedanticism, 'What was God doing with himself before the creation?' Moran is a recognisable human type who loses his certainties, his life of comfortable and secure habits, to end up much like Molloy, one of Beckett's many battered, handicapped specimens of humanity, who under their shabbiness and relative immobility can think intelligently without the barriers of conventional comforts and class mores. Molloy is a whole character, an outsider, who manages to look after himself well enough, existing somewhere between necessity and utility in Vico's scale of motivations. He has, after all, first a bicycle, then crutches, to help him to get around.

If the meaning of the novel, in terms of its descriptions of life, is clear, what can be said of the meaning of the parable? There can be little doubt that it is a parable, but it is neither neat nor clear. Molloy tells his story from his mother's bed, not sure how he managed to get there, certainly not with the help of Moran. At the end he is in a ditch, waiting for help, and the words come to him: 'Don't fret, Molloy, we're coming.' Is it Youdi whose voice he hears, telling him perhaps that Moran is on the way? If so, it is a forlorn hope. Beckett, if asked, would almost certainly say that he did not know what happened to get Molloy out of the ditch. If Moran is

Jesus, looking for man(kind), in order to save him, he is a willing, but totally incompetent 'saviour', and this would be a plausible Beckett comment. The nature of the work obliges the interested reader to keep looking for a key to break the code, but there may be not one code, but many. But even without that desire to know more, it remains a highly original novel, full of richly comic or grimly caustic incidents, written with a recognisable class-conscious social context where the Christian tradition, although much mocked by the author, is accepted by the characters. The novel belongs to the same world as *Waiting for Godot*, not to that of *Endgame* and the fictions that were to follow the *Trilogy*.

Malone Dies differs from *Molloy* in several ways. Stylistically it finds Beckett totally comfortable in his French writing, and having translated the novel unaided (*Molloy* had the not very welcome help of Patrick Bowles, who did a good job, but Beckett was never good at working with others), he found what he admitted was much pleasure in the work, 'childsplay' as he wrote to his American publisher, compared to *Molloy*. Even more than its predecessor, we can understand the richness of Malone's intelligent, thinking mind, unhampered by the presence and the company of others, especially when it becomes purely reflective, mingling its thoughts of the worrying present with his embroidered memories of the past and preparations for the sombre future. When writing *Proust*, Beckett, himself one of the friendliest of men when not totally absorbed in the work at hand, had already realised that solitude is a necessary precondition for true creativity.

> For the artist, who does not deal in surfaces, the rejection of friendship is not only reasonable, but a necessity. Because the only possible spiritual development is in the sense of depth. The artistic tendency is not expansive, but a contraction. And art is the apotheosis of solitude.[85]

Molloy is only occasionally solitary, although usually happiest when he is, but one feels he would like to be a social animal for part of the time, and he certainly enjoys getting drunk. But Malone is a floating mind in a dying body, grimly waiting for the end, telling himself stories, inventing or remembering—it is never quite clear which—other people, even whole families, like the Saposcats and the Lamberts. Malone invents his stories, by randomly casting about, the technique of nature, examining what he knows, what he does not know, reasoning out a little more, inventing where necessary. So he creates his character Sapo, giving him characteristics one by one, until he is recognisable, and once he has a picture of Sapo in his mind, the story begins to develop, and so do the other characters, his parents, siblings and acquaintances. Beckett makes many of his protagonists writers themselves so that through them he can convey something of his own difficulties and idiosyncrasies in producing his own work. In examining his own way of writing he is looking at the whole process of creation, because when he produces art the artist takes on the semblance and the role of God. Part of the Beckettian objection to art goes far beyond its function in making life more palatable for those wanting to escape from the horrors of worldly reality. It is because the artist is aping the creativity of God-Nature, endlessly expanding life and therefore the suffering it produces, that he finds a need to object. The creator must be the enemy. The very act of creating art is a reminder of the creation of life, and therefore evil by association. Schopenhauer came close to the same conclusion when he realised that the Will, which pushes all things forward, is itself evil.

In *Malone Dies* we are given an extraordinary series of metamorphoses. Malone develops in his mind the character and life of Sapo, who gets lost but is found again by his creator, becomes transformed into Macmann (son of man), a geriatric who undertakes a sexual coupling with Moll (a name close to Molloy), which contains more effort to achieve satisfaction than the satisfaction itself, let alone pleasure. Other characters, apparently from a lunatic asylum (a good enough metaphor for the world we inhabit) appear in Malone's invented tale until a grimmer figure, Lemuel, begins to kill them all, one by one. As Malone, through Lemuel, whom one may assume is a kind of demon from hell, removes his characters one by one, Malone himself appears to share their death; the last of his characters is about to drown when his consciousness peters out.

There are hints in *Malone Dies* that he, Malone, is a reincarnation of Molloy and perhaps of other, earlier Beckett heroes. Beckett's Malone is not, like Molloy, a character living in a recognisable 'real' world, that once bedridden he chronicles, but a creator, an artist, not a historian. As such he can indulge his fancies, create people, change them, change their names, their stories and lives, and suddenly move them from an urban or a rural environment into a lunatic asylum where different behaviour is normal. Beckett is therefore a creator creating a creator, who may create other creators, and destroyers as well. There is as much room in this scheme of things for fantasy, different realities, wish fulfilments, dreams of cruelty akin to de Sade's (whose work Beckett admired), as for a creative literature that aims at realism. Beckett is obviously, and deliberately, imitating God, whose creations are just as random, wild, cruel and destructive. If God is conscious of what he is doing, then he plays with us all, just as Malone plays with his own invented situations and characters, wiping them out when they bore him. 'What tedium' is as much God's feeling as Malone's.

The Unnamable, the third part of the *Trilogy*, is as different from *Malone Dies* as that novel is from *Molloy*. In *Molloy* we see God's world, and even if we cannot piece together the meaning of all the references to personalities that seem to have some biblical origin, we recognise the world of Molloy and Moran: it is the one in which we all live, seen first from the viewpoint of a bitter, observant and intelligent tramp, and then from that of a pedantic, God-fearing, middle-class private detective. The prevalence of detectives in Beckett's work is no accident. They do what philosophers do, look for what they do not know, often not sure of exactly what they are seeking. *Molloy* can be called novel about real life. *Malone* is a novel about a mind, in a dying body, creating: it is about the act of creation itself, and the only reality is the present circumstance of the narrator. *The Unnamable* is the crown of the *Trilogy*: a bodiless mind, a consciousness that may not be anchored in any body anymore. It may be the mind slowly fading out after the body has gone cold, a most likely hypothesis. Or it may be a mind that has left its body and is now waiting in limbo to be reincarnated into another body, almost as likely a supposition. Or it may be one of those voices that Vladimir hears, going over its life again in memory, rather less likely an explanation, because it is not its past life that interests it. Or it may be a soul in hell, or in limbo or purgatory. Any of these explanations fit the novel, a long rambling monologue that changes its tone frequently, but there is never a dull page in the work. It has grim humour, moments of pure terror, quieter reflective passages, periods of observation. It is the culmination of all of Beckett's outbursts, the monologues that started with Arsene's in *Watt*. It should be read slowly, and one can return to it endlessly.

The Unnamable, and we must assume that the noun applies to the speaker, who does not know who he is and would like to know, does not know where he is, but gives us nonetheless a good idea of what he perceives, was once alive, and something happened to him to end that life: 'You think you are simply resting the better to act when the time comes, or for no reason, and you soon find yourself powerless ever to do anything again.'[86] At the same time he seems to incorporate in his being all of Beckett's earlier protagonists, notwithstanding that they are also occasionally visible to him. It is as if the speaker were Beckett himself, or rather as if he were the author of all of Beckett's fictional writings, but of course invented by Beckett, a series of Chinese boxes of Russian dolls, all fitting within each other, the narrator being on the outside.

The Unnamable keeps changing his name, tells stories like Malone, seems to be rather like a genie that can inhabit anything or anyone he wants to. At one point he is Mahood, one of his own creations. Mahoud is the name of the novel in the original French version of *L'Innommable* and the spelling change is probably to aid pronunciation. Beckett's frequent image of the severed head emerges here for the first time. I have already pointed out that Beckett must have been aware of the grisly experiment carried out shortly after the war on two guillotined criminals, who, by prior agreement, had their heads interrogated after execution and were able to respond with their eyelids. This must have impressed itself deeply on Beckett because we get heads on jars talking to the audience in *Play*, a disembodied head in *Not I* and a not-quite-disembodied head in *That Time*. The other everyday image that links itself to the guillotined heads is the common restaurant advertisement that one sees all over France, a head on a jar, normally with a chef's hat and the menu hanging from its neck. This, at one point, is the situation of Mahood, inside a jar, armless and legless, an 'undeniable asset' for the restaurant owner. In later Beckett works, and indeed earlier in *Murphy*, Beckett frequently uses the image of the skull. It is of course the prison of the brain. But his skulls are sometimes inhabited by corpse-like figures, still alive, while the skulls become carriers, projectiles moving through space and time into eternity as if to probe the outer limits of the universe. The head and the skull are two of the most frequently used Beckett images.

In *The Unnamable* Beckett produces a whole new world of his own, rather as Swift did, and one certainly much influenced by Dante. Things that happen in our world happen there too, but the dead are alive, and those who were unable to move, like Malone, are mobile. There is memory of the past, both his own and other people's, and these others are his own creations. There are clues that at different times suggest the Unnamable might be Jesus, or God or the Devil, but there are also just as many statements that deny such interpretations. One thing certain is that the place where all these characters find themselves is eternal in the future, if not in the past.

> For I am obliged to assign a beginning to my residence here, if only for the sake of clarity. Hell itself, although eternal, dates from the revolt of Lucifer. It is therefore permissible, in the light of this distant analogy, to think of myself as being here forever, but not as having been here forever.[87]

It is not the purpose of this book to give explanations of the meanings behind Beckett's work, a task so many scholars have already undertaken, thoroughly sifting it. I have advanced Beckett's preoccupations and cited examples from the work where they shed light on the philosophy that emerges from them. The *Trilogy* has the universality to allow different readers to find in it what speaks to them most intimately. God is used as a metaphor for the author himself as the creator of his fictions, and to show that each fictional author has his own author creating him. The wonderful, but painful world of pure thought, speculation and observation, much of it in memory, is most potently embodied in *The Unnamable*, where the mind that talks belongs more to the world of scholastic philosophy than to any modern system of logic. Also the author is seen as a metaphor for God: he can create as much havoc as God does, depict the world according to whim and mood, exercise a taste for cruelty, or horror or for kindness and compassion if he chooses. The author is a troublemaker, like God. 'Yes, God, fomenter of calm, I never believed, not a second.'[88] And another point about the author's creations is that they will outlive him; they do not share his mortality. As with Hell, there was a time when they did not exist, but once in existence (and in print) there can be an assumption that they will always be there, long after the author has died and is only remembered by his words. Ultimately the author is only a voice, like The Unnamable, remembered by his recorded statements, bodiless and unseen. So, if God is dead, as Nietzsche proclaimed, it is through his handiwork that we still know him, because his words, that have come to us through the mouths of his prophets, especially Moses, Mohammed and Jesus, live on.

It will of course be obvious to any reader that in Hebrew theology God *is* the Unnamable, his name replaced by the letters J or Jehovah. As Yahweh, another version of the same name, he is mentioned in *The Unnamable*. But not too much should be made of this.

What interests so many serious Beckett readers is the ever-present interest in religious symbolism and dogma. God is never far out of sight, but we also know, from his own direct statements that Beckett was unable and unwilling to believe in any God or any doctrine or in a future life. Nonetheless, the 'perhaps' is still there. Beckett was not a dogmatic atheist.

An objective non-believer can often write about God and religion better than a believer, and certainly he can better portray those who believe. Shaw's *Saint Joan* is a good example of this, accurately depicting the conflict between faith as a bureaucratic system and faith as revelation, making the latter more convincing to an audience than the former, but enabling that audience to understand better the former as well. Beckett does this, not with Shaw's rationalism, but with the humility of the mystics, and the deep spirituality of Geulinex, whose self-denigratory attitudes were so close to his own. *Ubi nihil valis ibi nihil velis* meant, to Geulinex, that man must humble himself to his real value, which is nothing, in the knowledge of the enormous difference between himself and the greatness of God. But Beckett, while accepting the tinyness of man, turns the phrase into an act of defiance, a refusal to acquiesce in the design of nature for perpetual creation and growth, in order to be that nothing, but out of his own will. He told Laurence Harvey[89] that if he were a critic setting out to write about his own work that the Geulinex quotation was the best starting point, together with 'Nothing is more real than nothing' (Democritus). That *nothing* is the void before creation, the great emptiness that has to be filled, and it is Beckett's preoccupation with nothingness that caused him so often to be labelled an existentialist. That nothingness was the state of things before existence began and the beginning of God, or whatever we call the first cause, the state at which God is still acceptable, not yet having done any harm. Beckett has brooded long on the beginning of it all: perhaps the most important and unanswerable question is one he casually slipped in, as number thirteen, of the sixteen theological questions that Moran asks himself during the calvary of his homeward journey: 'What was God doing with himself before the creation?' Thirteen is a significant number for Beckett. When he uses it, one should take note. He was born on a Good Friday the thirteenth, but Joyce had the superstition before him. It comes, of course, from the Last Supper, thirteen at table, including Judas the betrayer. The problem of the *beginning* obsesses science and astronomy as much as theology. Was there a time when nothing happened? The trouble starts when God creates, when the void refuses to be void and begins to fill itself.

'On. Say on. Be said on. Somehow on. Till nohow on. Said nohow on.' So begins *Worstward Ho*, in which 'On', occurring as a key word in *Waiting for Godot*, *The Unnamable* and elsewhere, dominates almost every sentence. It is usually taken as an injunction, an encouragement, and to mean that whatever the vicissitudes one is undergoing, Beckett tells us never to give up, but to force ourselves to continue somehow. In a sense it does mean this, and represents the positive side of Beckett's thinking, and in his own life he adhered to it. But *On* is a paradox, because on the negative side it is not so much an injunction as something one cannot help. All nature forces things to go *On* and we are part of all things. We cannot *not* go On. That inability to let go, which would be much preferable to the continuing effort, is part of Beckett's protest. *On* is the will of God. Man should resist it, but cannot.

A key to Beckett's speculation about God lies in the middle part of the later *Trilogy*, in *Nohow On*, and in the novella *Ill Seen Ill Said*. Close reading brings out its secrets, because it does not have the ambiguity and the infuriating theological leads that peter out when one attempts to follow them, of *Molloy*, of which every commentator has in the end been forced to warn his readers to assume nothing concrete from them. In *Ill Seen Ill Said* we are dealing with a third-person monologue that imperceptibly, at the end, turns into first person. It is spoken with a forked tongue, but it tells a story, or rather it describes the end of a story, and it is as clear as Genesis. Its near biblical language hints at what it sets out to be, the last chapter of the bible.

It is God talking to himself, objectively, hiding from discovery, spying on an old woman who is both an individual and a collective entity out of mythology. The speaker is the God of Genesis and the Old Testament. He describes the old woman, now visible, now not, sitting at her window looking at Venus in the sky, or setting out on a mission outside her solitary cabin. He watches over her with pity, but remotely, without emotion. Things are happening in the area of the land around the cabin, the petrification of the world has begun, stones are overtaking vegetation. There are lambs in the fields but there is 'no trace of frolic'. The old woman is observed, not just by the eye of God, but by twelve guardians, sentinels on the horizon, who can only be the twelve apostles, and they watch over her. She goes to a slab, covering a grave. In the cabin a button-hook hangs on a nail; it is pisciform and the nail, 'unimpaired. All set to serve again. Like unto its glorious ancestors. At the place of the skull. One April afternoon.'[90] The atmosphere is that of a ghost story, which at times it is, while the watching eye loses her, finds her again, always anxious not to be discovered, occasionally admonishing itself: 'Careful.' Biblical and other references abound, but the main outline in clear. The tomb can only be that of Jesus. The widowed woman can only be the BVM, the Virgin Mary, which becomes clear from 'full of grace' quietly inserted on page 78 into the middle of a description of her spooning 'slop' from a bowl. She also appears to be Erda, the earth Goddess of many mythologies, but that is speculation.

Exact identification is not that important and the references have as much to do with the overtones of the New Testament as the actual text. What matters is the speaker, a conscious God, bored with his creations, who has brought into existence a world in which he now has little interest. The word in his mind is 'revoked'. He created the world, a great mistake, but can he now revoke that decision? Can he wipe out all of history, all the past as well as what exists now, all of time as well as all of space, all the worlds of his creation, including the perfect woman, the Virgin Mary, and her son, who is his, sent down to be also the son of man? The consequences will effect both Heaven and Hell because they too will go, must go if all of past history that sent the dead to an afterlife is revoked. Some will be relieved that their torment will end: 'Hear from here the howls of laughter of the damned.'[91]

In sentences of great, but not impenetrable obscurity; the

author shows God thinking out his destruction of the world, realising little by little that he has, perhaps, the power to do it. The vision of what he has created dims a little as he thinks about it.

> Ah the sweet one word. Less. It is less. the same but less. Whensoever the glare. True that the light. See now how words too. A few drops mishaphazard. Then strangury. To say the least. Less. It will end by being no more. By never having been. Divine prospect. True that the light.[92]

The light was of course created before the world, during the week of creation. That must go too. God prepares for the great work of total destruction; wiping out everything that has happened since his decision to create the world. The last two paragraphs of the novella are of great beauty, the joy of peace back in the void before creation began, and here the voice of the old woman, who will disappear in that return to the past of 'never having been', seems to be part of the joy of non-existence. At the last second God hesitates briefly, then accomplishes his revocation, back to the moment of his first, disastrous decision.

> Absence supreme good and yet. Illumination then go again and on return no more trace. On earth's face. Of what was never. And if by mishap some left then go again. For good again. So on. Till no more trace. On earth's face. Instead of always the same place. Slaving away forever in the same place. At this and that trace. And what if the eye could not? No more tear itself away from the remains of trace. Of what was never. Quick say it suddenly can and farewell say say farewell. If only to the face. Of her tenacious trace.

> Decision no sooner reached or rather long after than what is the wrong word? For the last time at last for to end yet again what the wrong word? Than revoked. No but slowly dispelled a little very little like the last wisps of day when the curtain closes. Of itself by slow millimetres or drawn by a phantom hand. Farewell to farewell. Then in that perfect dark foreknell darling sound pip for end begun. First last moment. Grant only enough remain to devour all. Moment by glutton moment. Sky earth the whole kit and boodle. Not another crumb of carrion left. Lick chops

and basta. No. One moment more. One last. Grace to breathe that void. Know happiness.[93]

Beckett's references are often deeply buried and tend to come to light when a reader suddenly spots a word in another text. The 'wrong word' *revoked* does not appear to have been previously spotted by the many Beckett scholars: it comes from Milton. Beckett found what he needed, in terms of language as well as concept, in Book III of *Paradise Lost*, where God, having raged against Satan for his revolt, and against Adam for the weakness he will show in the face of temptation, says

> Ingrate, he had of me
> All he could have; I made him just and right,
> Sufficient to have stood, though free to fall.[94]

Although dubious about his decision to give Man free will, God sticks to his decision, but also considers the alternative:

> I formed them free, and free they must remain,
> Till they enthral themselves; I else must change
> Their nature, and revoke the high decree
> Unchangeable, eternal, which ordained
> Their freedom, they themselves ordained their fall.[95]

This clears up a major difficulty in *Ill Seen Ill Said*, but Beckett is not Milton, and it is not free will he is talking about, but human existence. Whether this drastic decision by God is also a *Götterdämmerung* is not clear. God has presumably not also destroyed himself, and if he has not, the danger is that he may start again. He may get bored with breathing the void. *Ill Seen Ill Said* is of course no kind of theological or philosophical statement. It is a fictional, highly atmospheric and convoluted account of all of creation, based on Genesis, finding a useful echo in Milton, coming to an end by an act of will by the First Cause, whatever that is.

Beckett's next novella was about the creation of matter and man, *Worstward Ho*, and could suggest, just by its place in the canon, that a new creation of the world is what could happen next. Or it might be Genesis retold in more scientific and Beckettian term. The question is not important: the two short novels are complimentary; Beckett, having found a way for God to destroy the world, then went on to find a way to create it. But whether it is a first or a second creation, it is certainly *worstward*.

Beckett's lifelong thinking about God led him to finish his literary career by inventing a God able to realise the gravity of his mistake and powerful enough to correct it. In both these late works he had to develop two new prose styles of great power and dramatic eloquence, putting together a language almost as complex as the voices Moses heard in the burning bush. In a sense he is telling God what he might do to make amends, but warning us of what he might do again, unable to help himself. A conscious God seemed to Beckett to be unlikely, but he invented one. Beckett's various theological speculations, sometimes delivered as an aside, sometimes central to a particular text, all interlink. It seems difficult to believe that a man who uses so much religious material could be as agnostic as Beckett always insisted he was, but the paradox is true.

Man has always seen God in his own image. God is usually made to seem as like as possible to authority, a king, or leader of a nation or tribe, so that the divine authority becomes vested in the earthly one. Although Beckett was not political in the normal sense, he knew what authority was about, and he had no taste for tyranny, as his play *Catastrophe* amply attests. Although a society built on the principles of liberty, justice, conviviality, culture and universal security and pleasure is conceivable by the human mind, Utopia, in all the centuries recorded by history, has occasionally been glimpsed, but never achieved, and the glimpses are usually short. It is not God that has given us the greatest achievements of the human spirit at its best, but a few exceptional men and women. God, conscious or not, has only one function: to create. Man, having developed into an intelligent and conscious being, capable of much independence from his genetic structure—how much is still in dispute—has become a creator himself, usurping the function of God-Nature, able to give us a wealth of human inventions, many of them destructive, but also, through his development of a spiritual capacity (some of which is diverted into religious observance) a creator of art, making possible the masterworks of literature, music, painting, expressive movement and thought. Greedy man dominates the planet, but creative man feeds it: he will always be in a minority, and in any case creative man is not necessarily without greed. What Beckett makes clear is that it is not God, but man, who is occasionally spiritual, who has at least the capacity to be such. God is totally outside any spiritual existence or inspiration. God is pure materialism, striving eternally for growth. Capitalism, a system that grows through competitive destruction, and creates the misery of most for the benefit of the few, who think of themselves as Godlike, is very like the true nature of God. Put bluntly, God is Greed.

8

Prescriptions for Living: Beckett's Ethics

In his earliest published work of fiction, *More Pricks than Kicks*,[96] Beckett's hero, at the end of the first story, *Dante and the Lobster*, discovers that lobsters, thrown live into the pot, have a slow, painful and horrible death. His awareness that the animals we eat for food undergo similar suffering and terror turned him into almost a vegetarian, and Beckett did enjoy food; *almost*, because it is extremely difficult to be a vegetarian in France. Politeness was so important a part of his nature that he ate meat when it was put in front of him at a friend's house, but he never in later life ordered it in a restaurant, and in the old people's home where he ended his life, where meals were set, he took what was brought him, but picked out the vegetables, leaving the meat. He never complained or allowed friends to interfere with the establishment's routine by bringing in other food. Suffering, whether human or animal, was never far from his mind, and he knew that it was unavoidable for all that lives. The message that emerges most clearly from his work is that one should do whatever is possible to alleviate the suffering of others, and where possible prevent it, while ignoring one's own problems, whatever they might be, reducing by act of will one's own capacity to feel pain. But the most effective way to reduce suffering is to bring no new life into the world, thereby symbolically avoiding the mortal sin of Adam, which for Schopenhauer and Beckett—they use almost the same words—is procreation, not, as in Genesis, the acquisition of forbidden knowledge.

Beckett was able, as he advocated in *Proust*, to reduce his own desires but although he ignored pain, he obviously felt it, often physical pain from injuries received (he was accident-prone) and mental anguish. His correspondence with Thomas McGreevy, documented in Deidre Bair's biography,[97] tells us much about this anguish, obviously closely related to

his struggle to escape home, background and Irish Protestantism on the one hand, and on the other the effort to create
a form of literature that did not yet exist and might well be
beyond his powers. His spiritual pain was expressed most
poignantly in the early poetry, being part of a mystical search
that drove him to mental self-flagellation and near despair.
He never lost the sense of void left by abandoning the God
he was taught to love as a child, but loss of belief in no way
reduced his interest in religion and metaphysics. When inter-
viewed by Colin Duckworth in 1965 during rehearsals of *Waiting for Godot* at the Royal Court Theatre, and asked whether a
Christian interpretation of the play was justified, he answered:
'Yes, Christianity is a mythology with which I am perfectly
familiar. So naturally I use it.'[98] As Beckett speculated about
the creation of the world, he increasingly envisaged the
creator as a monster, but not necessarily a conscious one. The
only way to frustrate that God (or nature) was to produce no
children, and Beckett was true to his own principle. His attitude to children in general was always ambiguous. They were
alive through no fault of their own, but the sight of them sad-
dened him, and the anger that he might more logically have
directed towards their parents is occasionally transferred, not
seriously of course, to children themselves, because the kind-
est of men in life could be quite wicked in literature:

> ... till I had to fling myself to the ground to avoid crushing a
> child. He was wearing a little harness, I remember, with little
> bells, he must have taken himself for a pony, or a Clydesdale,
> why not. I would have crushed him gladly, I loathe children,
> and it would have been doing him a service, but I was afraid of
> reprisals. Everyone is a parent, that is what keeps you from
> hoping. One should reserve, on busy streets, special tracks for
> those nasty little creatures, their prams, hoops, sweets, scooters,
> skates, grandpas, grandmas, nannies, balloons and balls, all their
> foul little happiness in a word.[99]

It is of course the children of his own background that he
is describing, perhaps his own young self, and the words
come not from Beckett but from the jaundiced lips of one of
his fictional outcasts. But time and again he targets parents

as irresponsible criminals although, of course, in life courtesy prevented him from expressing his real feelings. Hamm denounces his parents in *Endgame* as 'accursed progenitors' and Molloy is bitterly unable to forgive his mother for bringing him into the world. In private I knew Beckett to express a passive anger at those who insisted in having families, however gloomy the future outlook, but in everyday life it is not possible to be both honest and logical in front of others who don't think about such things in terms of consequences and take a conventional view of life as a 'gift'.

In his writings we sometimes find a boy, seldom a girl, except where one is invented or remembered by one of his female characters on stage. The boy is nearly always the young Samuel Beckett himself, either as he remembered himself, or symbolically. The boy is pictured freshfaced and eager for the life ahead that he will find so different from expectation, and dominated by the ever-present knowledge of his own mortality.

One can make a personal decision to be childless, and it is usually the most responsible and sensitive members of the more affluent societies that make that decision. But once life is there, one has to resign oneself to it. Beckett talked much of suicide, but never seriously contemplated it as an immediate course of action. Those of his characters who talk about it never do it either. *Félo de se* is no answer, and as Beckett once said to me, it can leave a great mess for others. But, as Malone poignantly observes, for he is soon to die, once one is alive one might as well get on with it. And the only real answer to life, unsatisfactory perhaps, but practical, is to get what intellectual satisfaction one can out of an honest perception of reality, and to be kind and helpful to others. In this we find the heart of Beckett's ethics.

We must not forget that great as was his interest in all philosophy, it is the ethical thinkers who interested him most. And what attracted him to their thinking was the spirit of sacrifice, the deliberate belittling of the self and of personal needs in order to help others. Beckett was always aware of the problems of his friends, and people he knew only slightly,

sometimes not at all, would come to him for help. Where possible he was usually willing to drop whatever he was doing to
assist, although most of the time the need was simply for
money. When he did not have it, he would find a way to get it.

As a young man he turned himself into an unpaid, willing
slave for Joyce. During the war he sacrificed a career that was
poised to take off, and nearly his life as well, to support his
friends under the German Occupation, and he was a citizen
of a neutral country that never entered the war. After *Waiting
for Godot*, when his income had grown, he gave nearly all of
it away. Only Suzanne, his wartime companion, and late in
life his wife, knew how to spend on conventional things, but
modestly. To Beckett, the man of ideas, possessions were of
no interest, although he did buy a conventional apartment in
Paris, and later a small house in the country, where he could
work in peace. 'Things' did not interest him. His favourite
word in that respect was 'discard', and it certainly came easier
to him than to Hamm, who, with the end approaching, dis-
cards, one by one, his last few pathetic possessions. 'And
things, what is the correct attitude towards things?' asks the
Unnamable on the second page of the novel, and he goes on

> And, to begin with, are they necessary? . . . If a thing turns up,
> for some reason or another, take it into consideration. Where
> there are people, it is said, there are things. Does this mean that
> when you admit the former you must also admit the latter?[100]

In so far as things were important to other people, Beckett
often helped them to get what they wanted with money.
When, as part of the Nobel Prize for Literature, he was
awarded a large sum, tax free, he gave every penny away
within a few weeks. I was one, perhaps of many, whom he
consulted. How could the money best be used? By the time I
had compiled a list of aspiring writers whose work would
benefit from a modest donation to relieve pressing debts, it
was all gone. Some of the demands made directly to Beckett
were obviously not so modest, because the entire amount—I
never knew exactly how much the prize money was—went
out in a very short time. By normal standards Beckett's gen-

erosity often smacked of folly, but that did not worry him. He could recognise a knave, but held no prejudice against those whose standards were lower than his own. There is no record of where the money went. Beckett often helped to finance the artistic ventures of his friends, paid the university fees of a number of needy students who came to him, and helped others with their debts. No successful writer of whom I have heard has ever kept so little of his earnings for himself. When he died there was little in the bank and a tax debt for his heirs to pay. Like Saint Francis of Assisi, with whom he shared so many traits, he would gladly have given his cloak to someone worse off than himself.

Much published work would never have seen the light of day in his lifetime had it not been for someone's special need. Beckett withheld many texts because he was dissatisfied with them, but he would on occasion overcome his reluctance to publish to help someone else. His very last prose text, *Stirrings Still*, was written at the appeal of his long-time American publisher Barney Rosset, who, having been forced by economic circumstances to sell his company, was ousted from it. His appeal was for some new text to keep the connection symbolically alive. Beckett, having decided he would write no more, then produced a last late masterpiece. To do for others what he would not do for himself was, for Samuel Beckett, perfectly normal behaviour. As a man and as an artist he was as near to a saint as anyone I have ever met.

Examples of Beckett's kindness to others, even to stray people he met on the street, often to those with whom he could have nothing in common other than human kinship, became legends. Once, in Paris, he was stopped for assistance by two Irish labourers on holiday, not knowing what to do with their time or where to go. He took them, perfect strangers, but fellow countrymen, out for the best evening of their lives, which included dinner and a night-club about which he had heard but never visited, one of the most expensive in Paris. Only later, back in Dublin, knowing his name, did they discover who their generous host had been. Another anecdote, which I have from the Irish ambassador, concerns the occasion when Beckett went to the consulate in Paris to renew his passport. Sitting waiting, next to a tourist who had been mugged and had not eaten for a day, Beckett gave him all he had in his pocket and sent him out to eat, only to find that he could not pay for his passport or his bus home. He was always a good companion to others.

There is Cain and Abel in all of us. Beckett could snap back when tormented, especially when badgered by journalists and photographers, and turn savage like a cornered beast when his privacy was threatened by celebrity hunters or those whom he recognised as greedy and unscrupulous exploiters of his work. France is the best country for a well-known person who wishes to be left alone, and he was only very occasionally bothered there. Some journalists became personal friends; they respected his privacy and agreed to print nothing that fell from his lips or write about him during his lifetime. Most of them did after he died. When he felt betrayed, he dropped that person from his acquaintanceship.

Beckett's strictures in *Proust* on friendship must be taken in their proper context. In fact it is Proust talking, not Beckett, when he says that 'Friendship implies an almost piteous acceptance of face values . . . a social experiment', and that 'the rejection of friendship is not only reasonable, but a necessity'. Beckett, whose own need for solitude was as great as Proust's, well understood the French novelist's point that 'Friendship is the negation of that irremediable solitude to which every human being is condemned', but he did not share Proust's essential egotism. He had to be alone to write, but he did not want to be alone or to be writing all the time. He had a need for friendship as relief, and much of it he found in his practical work in the theatre, in the company of actors rehearsing his work for performance. He was always himself a true and loyal friend and wonderful company, and some of his friends were companions as well. The distinction is important, and is brought out in such texts as *Company*, where, as in life, companions eventually disappear, and one is ultimately left alone.

Beckett's generosity, with his time as well as his means, brought him many problems. There were those who wanted to meet him in order to be able to boast of their intimacy and others who wrote him on various pretexts in order to get letters back, either to sell them later or get their names into literary history. He endured all that with no complaint, knowing well enough what the motives were. The whole concept of friendship and companionship is crucial to his view of life and his moral stance. Both, but especially the latter, is essential to his work, where companionship is the only effective shield against a hard and grasping world, indifferent to the needs of those who have nothing. In *Waiting for Godot*, in *Mercier and Camier*, and in those works where the relationship between two people is not an equal one, like those of Pozzo and Lucky, and Hamm and Clov, the bond is almost as great, because it consists of a mutual dependence. Beckett had many prewar close friends, and with some of them he corresponded regularly, needing a sympathetic ear and practical advice. Because of that correspondence, especially with Thomas McGreevy, we know of his mental distress and the psychosomatic medical problems they induced. With *Waiting for Godot* came fame and self-sufficiency, and he no longer needed friends for moral support and to share his anxieties. The number of people forcing themselves on him had by then become an encumbrance, especially obtrusive journalists, and his real friends, many now dead or far off in Ireland, were few. But they included professional colleagues, producers and actors, including Roger Blin, George Devine and Alan Schneider, all of whom staged his plays according to his wishes, and he still knew many visual artists from the old days like Giacometti and William Hayter, and new ones, Joan Mitchell, Rosset's first wife, the Israeli artist Avigdor Arikha, Sorel Etrog from Romania, and visitors from London like Barbara Bray, Martin Esslin and Harold Pinter. These were the people with whom he could relax, conversational and drinking companions. The fish restaurants and cafés of Montparnasse knew him well. Disappointed journalists, frozen out and refused interviews, described him as a recluse, but he was far from reclusive with his friends.

The solitude that a writer needs has to be organised, and it was eventually at Ussy on the Marne that he did most of his real work, rationing out his time, spending weeks alone, thinking and writing, sometimes visiting Henri and Josette Hayden, who had been his fellow refugees at Roussillon during the war, who lived only a few miles away, then returning to Paris for a week to lunch and dine with friends and visitors, with an occasional late-night or all-night session. He had sexual needs too of course, but that is for his biographers to investigate; Peggy Guggenheim and others have written about his sexual nature, and there is no need to say more. In old age, Beckett would meet friends and others in the café of an hotel across the street from his Paris apartment, always arriving punctually, as he had all his life, and leaving exactly when he had pre-decided to leave. Later still, in the retirement home where he ended his days, he was vulnerable to anyone who walked in, but fortunately few people knew where it was. This rather long digression is to explain how a man who allowed so many people to take advantage of him and utilise his time, could still function as a writer and at the highest level of achievement. When he had to be alone, he simply took himself out of the way.

The difference between friendship and comradeship is evident in Beckett's writing, and the distinction is important. The first can be deep or skin-deep and depends mainly on liking and common interests. Friends must enjoy each other's company, but such friendships are not an absolute necessity in life. Friendship is a gift not given to everyone, and it is often rare among those who have achieved, and are continuing to achieve, worldly success. A companion is someone with whom we might have little in common, but whom one needs, and on whom one can rely. A companion will not easily give away one's name under torture. Companionship is a bond forged by hardship and common experience. Friends are in Beckett's work; the many pseudo-couples are really companions. A companion is a need, a friend, a relaxation.

> What would I do what I did yesterday and the day before
> peering out of my deadlight looking for another
> wandering like me eddying far from all the living[101]

The lines would seem to suggest the need for love, and perhaps that is what companionship is really about, a love created by experience and need. The three lines are from a group of poems written in French during the 'siege' years of *Waiting for Godot* and the *Trilogy*; much of what is portrayed in them is the need and search for companionship, or the lack of it, which is real solitude, such as we find in the narratives of Molloy and Malone, and the power of the solitary exploring mind to float in free thought as if it had escaped the restraints of the body. About love in the physical sense, Beckett is always caustic:

> It was she made me acquainted with love. She went by the peaceful name of Ruth I think, but I can't say for certain. Perhaps the name was Edith. She had a hole between her legs, oh not the bunghole I had always imagined, but a slit, and in this I put, or rather she put, my so-called virile member, not without difficulty, and I toiled and moiled until I discharged or gave up trying or was begged by her to stop. A mug's game in my opinion and tiring on top of that, in the long run. But I lent myself to it with a good enough grace, knowing it was love, for she had told me so.[102]

So much for physical love! Beckett knew perfectly well what love and sex was, but in his mind he could never dissociate the latter from its likely consequence in procreation, and he also knew that love based on physical attraction is seldom durable. Companionship, even with a degree of tension built into it, does endure. Beckett's long relationship with Suzanne, whom he only married late in life after many years of living together, including the wartime years in hiding, was one of companionship. There is no stronger crutch for the wearying journey of life.

A service that Beckett has done for many is to take away their fear of inadequacy. The pressure of education, of parents and of society itself to be successful, an achiever, a person of means and power, is always great. The purpose of such ambition can only be itself. The visibly successful person always sees him- or herself through the eyes of others: such people can seldom be on their own for long, needing the constant attention and admiration of others. The very effort of achieving something in the world tends to inhibit the ability to ask *Why* and any desire to find a meaning or purpose to the effort, other than self-aggrandisement. As we are all mortal any achievement is certain to crumble into dust, or at least to be lost to the individual who achieves it. The situation is different for art. Artists can only create out of the very faculties that are inhibited in others, the ability to perceive, think, feel and understand. But the true artist never has a real sense of achievement, his creation always in his own eyes falling short of what he is seeking. The artist, however, cannot be deterred: his goal is not arrival, but the journey. He will undergo whatever hardship is necessary to work at his art. As such he is usually happier than the person striving to be rich or richer, or to increase his power and authority, because he does not share their constant anxiety. The demand of art is total concentration which, temporarily at least, submerges worry. The artist also accepts failure better, indeed as Beckett put it, 'Failure is his world'.

The artist is always a case apart, a man who lives by facing the reality that most other go to great pains to avoid. Modern industrial society, where desires, hopes and ambitions are artificially created by a massive public relations and advertising industry, portraying every aspect of life in unrealistic and glowing terms, persuades the public not to look and not to think. Its product is hedonism and it makes it easy to avoid reality until the moment of truth arrives: the loss of one's livelihood, the repossession of a mortgaged home, severe illness or painful death.

Beckett is not only talking to artists in the message obliquely woven into his work, but saying, to as much of humanity as will listen, that if it can learn to forego personal ambition and think in terms of co-operation, compassion and companionship, it will be happier. It would in fact be moving closer to the condition of the artist. For the awareness of tragedy, which does not come easily to most people, makes nonsense of self-aggrandisement and the mythology of success. Greater ability should be used to further the happiness, however temporary, of all members of society, not temporarily to elevate the person who possess it over the rest.

Human nature is such that Beckett does not really believe this is possible—all human wish-dreams have ultimately turned out to be hollow—but the 'perhaps' is still there. It is a tiny glimmer of hope, but better than nothing. Any discussion of methods of achieving such a just and good society would lead us into the realm of political theory, which Beckett always avoided, even in discussion. His reasons can be found principally in an instinctive, deeply rooted objection to social engineering accomplished by institutions. It smacked too much of Victorian charity, and it diverted attention away from the incurable ills of humanity, the tragedy of its existence. He was aware of, but not very interested in the Welfare State, when it existed, because he did not think it would last, and he was right. In this one instance his outlook was similar to Margaret Thatcher's: he believed that one can only understand and help the individual. His well-known disinterest in social progress had many foundations, one of them his irritation at critics like Kenneth Tynan, who could not divorce their aesthetic sense from their social philosophy and saw art largely in sociorealistic terms, while others were founded in his conviction, based on accurate observation, that man's atavistic and selfish nature was too strong a match for his idealism. The demiurge is not on the side of virtue. But there always remains some hope in our ability to protest and to curse our lot: 'A pox on void'.

It is clear that Beckett, as a reader of philosophy, and an independent thinker himself, carried on the thinking of the stoics and the pessimistic philosophers from the medieval mystics to Heidegger, giving ideas a concrete form in his novels and plays. He grew up a generation later than the Bloomsbury writers and painters, whose guru was G. E. Moore. Beckett must have been aware of Moore, but it would be difficult to think of an ethical philosopher more opposed to his own thinking. Moore was the ultimate epicurian, a hedonist for whom beauty and pleasure were the only motives for action and life. Moore admired mental qualities, but believed they were worthless without material qualities to support them. In defining the idea, Moore also defined its opposite:

> Great evils may be said to consist either (a) in the love of what is evil or ugly, or (b) in the hatred of what is good or beautiful, or (c) in the consciousness of pain.[103]

Moore was very much a product of the Edwardian age, which to the financially comfortable educated classes still glitters like a golden age, like the age of Raphael in the Renaissance and that of Europe before the French Revolution. Two world wars have given us a new perspective on evil, and with it the work of Picasso, Giacometti and Bacon, of Kafka, Brecht and Beckett, of Bartok and Berg. Moore would have classed these under all three of his categories. Since his time we have learned to see beauty in decay and comfort in the acceptance of pain. No rational person can deny that the message of the pessimistic thinkers and artists of our time have at least as much to offer us aesthetically as their predecessors, and that they more accurately depict the world we inhabit and the lives we lead. Nevertheless Moore, in his much later second preface to the *Principia*, (not published until 1993, thirty-five years after his death), by accepting the subjectivity of the concept of 'Goodness' moved a little in the direction that Beckett was to take.

Beckett's ethics cannot be directly quoted, only deduced. They are not clearly stated because of the overwhelming pessimism underlying his thinking, which has its roots in the failure of monotheism to explain the malignity of the world and the contradictions between what it preaches and what it practices. Beckett certainly looked closely at pantheism. But as Schopenhauer points out, ethics is bound to be lost in any pantheistic view of the world, because 'the difference between right and wrong, and in general between good and evil' becomes 'hollow and empty',[104] a convention. Buddhism in particular, with its concept of justice in nature through rebirth, so that one may expect the suffering inflicted on others in this life to be inflicted in kind on ourselves in the next, did not appeal to either Schopenhauer or Beckett, and it is far from the transcendental pantheism where all things continue to exist through a never-ending metamorphosis into something else. Schopenhauer's ethical metaphysics are based on three principles:[105] compassion or *caritas*, the basis of justice and philanthropy; *amor*, which includes sexual love, and is superior to egoism, the love of oneself; and *magic*, the art of healing and of persuasion, the magnetism of the prophets and those secular leaders who had led their followers to higher principles of living. Of course all three have their opposites, selfishness, hate and envy, and megalomania, leading others towards evil. Beckett, in his own way, and in his own language, echoes those Schopenhauerian principles, showing each in its ideal light through the catharsis his work imposes on his readers and audiences, while portraying, with the power only a great writer can command, how the evil manifestations of selfishness, hate and megalomania, make our world the misery that it is.

Much has been said about Beckett's charity. For *amor* we can read that love that is embodied in compassion and companionship, while the magic lies in his genius, his power over words.

One of the great errors by which we live, in spite of all the evidence to the contrary, is that the purpose of life is happiness. Although G. E. Moore is almost forgotten, his ethics, in a more popular form, survive, but they can have no validity in a world bent on self-destruction. And his views were purely secular, unlike those which promise an after-life and also promise that if happiness, for whatever reason, is not possible in this life, that we shall achieve it in the next. The political expediency in the 'pie in the sky' argument is obvious enough, as is the religious necessity for it, but it too does not hold much credibility today. If anything the classical descriptions of the world across the Styx, on which Dante heavily leaned, for he had little available in Christian mythology, is both more aesthetically satisfying and interesting, but not credible either. We are born, we live, and we die. In all this is the Will of nature, the Omni-Omni as the Unnamable calls it, and nature passes on that Will to all living things. Our purpose seems to be nothing more than to become a link in the chain whereby the creative impulse, or our DNA as we now know it to be chemically, is passed on to future life. Shaw, an optimist, saw hope of some kind in the future, when man would become God-like. Kafka saw the possibility of something brighter in the future, but no more than that. Proust found his peace in the golden glow of the remembered past, an experience common to most people who live to a comfortable old age. To Beckett life was the short straw of existence that those of us who are born are unlucky enough to draw. We live, as Vladimir says, until we die and are forgotten. If there is an answer to life, it must be in *caritas*, a human willingness to share, to comfort, to be a good companion.

And, of course, we need two other things, and we find them both in Beckett: the courage of the stoics, who trained themselves to face without flinching that which is inevitable; and secondly, the wisdom to discard, not only the vanities of the world and the love of possessions, but our own sense of personal value. We can be grateful, because it is a panacea (and this is the present author talking, not Beckett) for the things we have recognised as interesting, beautiful and life-enhancing, that have made the burden a little easier, but they have no ultimate value in the immensity of time and space, and neither have any of us. Sadly, that even applies to Beckett himself, the producer of great aesthetic pleasure that has been a catharsis to his admirers everywhere.

Beckett's most important work shows us how to face and accept the inevitable and the importance of doing it with dignity. Seneca told Lucilius that the best way to avoid the fear of death was never to stop thinking about it. We know that we shall be nothing in the future, just as we were nothing in the past. We must also accept that we are nothing in the present, looked at by the eye of time, but that does not stop us from doing something, which may help others to endure their existence a little better, and through the realisation of their own nothingness, go on to help still others in the same way. Only when that realisation sinks in can we finally re-enter the void from which we came and the peace where there is 'Nohow on'.

ENDNOTES

1. Samuel Beckett, *Proust*, London, 1965, p. 18.

2. Arnold Geulincx (1625–69): Belgian philosopher, whose *Ethica* was published in 1665.

3. Belacqua, a real life Florentine character known to Dante, suffers in purgatory because of his extreme torpidity and unwillingness to do anything other than grow wise by resting and thinking.

4. Lance St John Butler, *Beckett and the Meaning of Being*, London, 1984.

5. Although I had this reference when the book was written, I was unable to recover it at a later date.

6. T. S. Eliot, '*Sweeny Agonistes*' in *the Complete Poems and Plays of T. S. Eliot*, London, 1969, p. 122.

7. Je suis ce cour de sable qui glisse, in *Collected Poems 1930–1979*, London, 1984.

8. Bertrand Russell, *What I Have Lived For*, introduction to Autobiography, London.

9. *Worstward Ho*, London, 1983, p. 9.

10. See *Molloy, Malone Dies, The Unnamable*, London, 1959, pp. 66–77.

11. His wife Suzanne whom he married in 1962, had more conventional standards and her Paris apartment, joined at the back to Sam's, was well-furnished in contrast to the austerity of his.

12. *From an Abandoned Work* in *Six Residua*, London, 1978, p. 19.

13. *Disjecta*, edited by Ruby Cohn, London, 1983, p. 52 (German), pp. 171–2 (English).

14. Comment by the author when discussing producing the first post war edition.

15. *Murphy*, London, 1977, p. 63. This reference applies initially to Bishop Berkeley, but it is equally relevant to Kant.

16. Ibid.

17. *Murphy*, p. 66.

18. Ibid.

19. *Company*, London, 1980, pp. 54–5.

20. *Molloy, Malone Dies, The Unamable*, London, 1959. See Note 5.

21. *Proust*, London, 1965, p. 67.

22. Letter to Tom Driver in *Beckett by the Madeleine*, Columbia University Forum, Summer 1961.

23. *Watt*, part 1, London, 1963, p. 47.

24. Roughly translated by J. Calder as 'Look at the worst / laugh till you burst'.

25. In Beckett's darkest play, which was also his favourite, *Endgame*, we get another boy, but here the message is different. He symbolises the possibility of life in the future, whereas Clov, who sees the boy in the distance through a spyglass, is hoping that the world is dying and all life with it. This is one of the few Beckett works where the need to be recognised does not seem to be present. Nevertheless Hamm, observed, although he thinks he is alone and totally abandoned by the Clov who is about to depart but may not, plays out his last piece of theatre to himself, regaining his dignity for his last struggle with death.

26. *Watt*, London, 1963, p. 153.

27. Ibid.

28. David Hume, *A Treatise of Human Nature*, Edinburgh, 1739.

29. *Worstward Ho*, London, 1983, pp. 46–7.

30. *Molloy, Malone Dies, The Unnamable*, London, 1959, p. 71.

31. The tumour, fortunately, turned out to be benign and was removed some years later.

32. Molloy, in *Molloy, Malone Dies*, The Unnamable, London, 1959, p. 24.

33. Ibid., p. 67.

34. *First Love*, London, 1973, pp. 32–3.

35. *Company*, London, 1980, pp. 17–18.

36. John Pilling, *Samuel Beckett*, London, 1976.

37. *Molloy, Malone Dies, The Unnamable*, London, 1959, p. 19.

38. *Waiting for Godot*, Act II, London, 1956, pp. 90–1.

39. *Proust*, London, 1965, p. 60.

40. Molloy in *Molloy, Malone Dies, The Unnamable*, London, 1959, p. 58.

41. See 'Song' in *Collected Poems*, London, 1984.

42. *Collected Poems*, London, 1986, p. 41.

43. *Worstward Ho*, London, 1983.

44. *Proust*, London, 1965, p. 12.

45. Ibid., p. 15.

46. Ibid., p. 15.

47. Ibid., p. 15.

48. Ibid., p. 18.

49. Ibid., p. 36.

50. Ibid., p. 31.

51. Ibid., p. 31.

52. Ibid., p. 31.

53. Ibid., p. 18.

54. Ibid., p. 33.

55. *Proust*, Ibid., p. 74.

56. *Lessness*, paragraph 3.

57. *Proust*, p. 78.

58. In my conversations with Beckett I came to realise his deep knowledge and understanding of Kafka's major works.

59. *Proust and Three Dialogues with Georges Duthuit*, London, 1965, pp. 102–3.

60. Ibid., p. 103.

61. Ibid., p. 110.

62. Ibid., p. 113.

63. Ibid., p. 190.

64. *Fingal*, the second story.

65. Christopher Ricks, *Beckett's Dying Words*, Oxford, 1993.

66. Bertrand Russell, *An Enquiry into Memory and Truth*, London, 1940.

67. Ludwig Wittgenstein, *Philosophical Investigations*, Oxford, 1953.

68. *Waiting for Godot*, London, 1956, pp. 52 and 62 respectively. Note the rhyme of *dies* and stage direction *sighs* (unheard by the audience) and the *Afterthought*. (The theme of being remembered: Christ's crucifixion accomplished that for him). Reading the text as well as hearing it is necessary to get all of Beckett's finer points.

69. Friedrich Heer, *The Intellectual History of Europe*, London, 1966.

70. *Collected Poems*, London, 1984, pp. 58–9.

71. *Complete Dramatic Works*, London, 1986, p. 256.

72. Molloy in *Molloy, Malone Dies, The Unnamable*, London, 1959, p. 19.

73. *How It Is*, London, 1964, p. 117.

74. All dates given are of first publication in the original language of composition.

75. 'Old Earth' in *For to End Yet Again*, London, 1976, p. 54.

76. *Selected Poems*, London, 1999.

77. *Worstward Ho*, London, 1983, p. 8.

78. Dante . . . Bruno. Vico . . . Joyce in *Our Exagmination Round his Factification for Incamination of Work in Progress*, Paris, 1929, *Transition*, No. 16–17 and in *Disjecta*, London, 1983.

79. Giambattista Vico, *The Third New Science* (Translated from the Italian by Leon Pompa), London.

80. *Disjecta*, London, 1983, p. 27.

81. *The Way*. Still unpublished.

82. John Fletcher, *The Novels of Samuel Beckett*, London, 1964, p. 120. All the above works were written in French. Titles given are those of the English translations.

83. Ibid., p. 125.

84. *Malone Dies* in *Molloy, Malone Dies, The Unnamable*, London, 1959, pp. 222–3.

85. *Proust*, London, 1965, p. 64.

86. *The Unnamable*, in *Molloy, Malone Dies, The Unnamable*, London, 1959, p. 293.

87. Ibid., p. 298.

88. Ibid., p. 307.

89. *Samuel Beckett: Poet and Critic*, Princeton, 1970.

90. *Ill Seen Ill Said*, London, 1981, p. 95.

91. Ibid., p. 54.

92. Ibid., p. 52.

93. Ibid., p. 59.

94. *Paradise Lost*, Book III, lines 97–90.

95. Ibid., lines 124–80.

96. *More Pricks than Kicks*, London, 1970.

97. *Samuel Beckett, A Biography*, London, 1978.

98. Colin Duckworth, *Angels of Darkness*, London, 1972, p. 18.

99. *The Expelled* in *Four Novellas*, London, 1977, p. 39.

100. *The Unnamable*, in *Molloy, Malone Dies, The Unnamable*, London, 1959, p. 294.

101. 'Que ferai-je / What would I do' in *Collected Poems 1930–1978*, London, 1998, p. 61.

102. *Molloy* in *Molloy, Malone Dies, The Unnamable*, London, 1959, p. 56.

103. G. E. Moore, *Principia Ethica*, Revised Edition, London, 1993, p. 273.

104. Arthur Schopenhauer, *The World as Will and Representation*, Chapter 10.

105. Ibid., Chapter XLVIII (*On Ethics*).

Bibliography

Works by Samuel Beckett

NOVELS

Dream of Fair to Middling Women
More Pricks Than Kicks
Murphy
Watt
Mercier and Camier
First Love
Molloy
Malone Dies
The Unnamable
How It Is
Company
Ill Seen Ill Said
Worstward Ho

SHORT PROSE FICTION

Three Novellas (The Expelled, The Calmative, The End)
Texts For Nothing
From An Abandonned Work
All Strange Away
Enough
Imagination Dead Imagine
Ping
Lessness
The Lost Ones
For to End Yet Again (Fizzles)
(For to End Yet Again, Still, He is Barehead, Afar A Bird, Horn Came Always, I Gave Up Before Birth, Closed Space, Old Earth)
As The Story Was Told (As The Story Was Told, Heard In The Dark, One Evening, Neither)
Stirrings Still
What Is The Word

PLAYS

Human Wishes
Eleutheria
Waiting For Godot
Krapp's Last Tape
Endgame
Happy Days
All That Fall
Act Without Words I
Act Without Words II
The Old Tune (adapted from Pinget)
Embers
Words and Music
Come and Go
Breath
Rough for Radio I
Rough for Radio II
Rough for Theatre I
Rough for Theatre II
Cascando
Play
Eh Joe
Ghost Trio
. . . but the clouds . . .
Not I
Rockaby
Footfalls
That Time
Ohio Impromptu
Piece of Monologue
Quad
Catastrophe
What Where
Nacht und Träume
What Where

CRITICISM

Proust and Three Dialogues with Georges Duthuit
Disjecta

POETRY

Collected Poems
Selected Poems

FILM SCENARIO

Film

About Beckett

The number of books written about Samuel Beckett reputedly come sixth in the world bibliography, after Jesus, Napoleon, Beethoven, Wagner and James Joyce, all iconic figures who have attracted a large cult. The small number given here have been useful for this book, but are listed mainly because they will also be helpful to those who read it.

Calder, John. As No Other Dare Fail. Calder, London 1988
Cronin, Anthony. Samuel Beckett, The Last Modernist. Collins, London 1996
Harvey, Lawrence. Samuel Beckett, Poet and Critic. Princeton Univ. Press, Princeton 1970
Knowlson, James. Damned to Fame. The Life of Samuel Beckett. Bloomsbury, London 1996
Knowlson & Pilling. Frescoes of the Skull. Calder, London 1979
McMillan & Flhsenfeld. Beckett in the Theatre. Calder, London 1988
Peter, John. Vladimir's Carrot. Univ. of Chicago Press, Chicago 1987
Pilling, John. Samuel Beckett. Routledge, London 1976
Revue d'Esthetique. Beckett. Privat, Paris 1986
Ricks, Christopher. Beckett's Dying Words. Clarendon Press, Oxford 1993

INDEX

À la Recherche de temps perdu
  Abel 89, 113–14
Act Without Words 2 44, 115
Adam 24, 25, 41, 53, 129
All That Fall 96
Angels of Darkness 146
Arikha, Avigdor 135
Aristotle 32, 58
Arsene (*Watt*) 29, 31, 40, 119
Arthur (*Watt*) 39
Arts Theatre Club 98
Assumption 35
Bair, Deidre 16, 129
Baudelaire, Charles 114
Beatrice (Dante) 58
Beckett and the Madeleine 143
Beckett and the Meaning of Being 143
Beckett, Suzanne 132, 137
Beckett's Dying Words 145
Beethoven, Ludwig van 7, 98, 107
Belacqua 5, 22, 25, 28, 86
Bergson, Henri 109
Berkeley, Bishop 4, 19, 29, 42
Bérenger 30
Bildungsroman 64
Blin, Roger 135
Boulevard St. Jacques 12
Brahma 3
Bray, Barbara 135
Breath 9, 16
Breton, Andre 75
Brod, Max 80
Bruno, Giordano 104
Buddhism 5, 43
Bunyan, John 113
Butler, Lance St. John 6
. . . *but the clouds* . . . 101
Caesar 104

Cain 89, 113–114
Camier 51, 57
Cartesian Philosophy 39, 62
Catastrophe 127
Cathars 40
Celia (*Murphy*) 26, 46
Chambermaid (*Molloy*) 58
Christ 90, 113
Christian (*Pilgrim's Progress*) 113
Christianity 14, 91–2, 106
Christian mystics 6
Christina, Queen 63
Citizen Kane 68
Clov (*Endgame*) 24, 57, 60, 135
Coat, Tal 78
Cohn, Ruby 143
Collected Poems (SB) 144
Comment c'est 98
Commonplace Book 38
Company 53, 69–70, 102, 134
Coupole, La 109
Criterion, Theatre 98
Dante 4, 5, 15, 22, 25, 43, 58, 69, 91,
  99, 103, 109, 113, 121, 141
Dante . . . Bruno. Vico . . . Joyce 145
Dante and the Lobster 129
Dasein 30
Darwin, Charles 19, 92
Death and the Maiden 97
Democritus 122
Descartes, Rene de 4, 14, 18, 19, 24,
  32, 37, 40, 62–3
The Devil 41, 72, 121
Devine, George 135
Dickens, Charles 60
Disjecta 143
Divine Comedy 91
Dream of Fair to Middling Women 5,
  18

Driver, Tom 143
Dualism 24, 33, 43
Duckworth, Colin 130
Dún Laoghaire 61
Duthuit, Georges 78–80
Eliot, T. S. . 2, 8, 45
Eleutheria 110
Embers 96
Endon, Mr (*Murphy*) 25, 26
Endgame 8, 60, 72, 98, 116
Enough 90, 99
Enquiry into Memory and Truth 145
Erda 57
Eroica, The 98
Estragon (Waiting for Godot) 3, 24,
    41, 51, 53, 56–7, 60, 73, 90–1
Esslin, Martin 17, 98, 135
Ethica (Geulincx) 4
Etrog, Sorel 135
Falstaff, The 109
Film 29
Finnegan's Wake 18, 103
First Love 53, 55
Fizzles 101
Fletcher, John 110
Footfalls 36, 97, 101
For to End Yet Again 99, 101
Gaber 112
Gadafi 11
Geulincx, Arnold 4, 5, 24, 33, 40, 65,
    122
Ghost Trio 35, 36, 101
Giacametti, Alberto 135
Gideon 28
Godot 3, 28, 34, 71, 106
Goethe, J. W. von 42, 64
Guggenheim, Peggy 136
Hamlet 10, 34
Hamm (Endgame) 8, 24, 57, 60, 63,
    72, 102, 135
Hammerklavier Sonata 98
Happy Days 51, 57, 97
Harvey, Laurence 122
Harzreise in Winter 42
Hayden, Henri 50, 135
Hayden, Josette 136

Hayter, William 135
Heer, Friedrich 93
Heidegger 6, 30, 43, 139
Henry V 10
heresy 6
Higgins, Aidan 86
Hobson, Harold 12
How It Is 27, 36, 46, 98–9
Huit clos 35
Hume, John 19, 20, 42
Hussein, Saddam 11
Idealism 19
Ill Seen Ill Said 73, 102, 123–127
Imagination Dead Imagine 22, 42, 44,
    90, 99
Inferno 5, 113
L'Innomable 119
Ionesco, Eugene 30
Jacques (*Molloy*) 111
Jehova 121
Jesus 111, 116, 121
Joan of Arc 107, 122
Jolas, Eugene 78
Joseph 111
Joyce, James 1, 2, 6, 17, 20, 48, 49,
    98, 103–5, 112, 122, 132
Joyce, Lucia 96
Judaism 14
Jung, Karl 96
Kafka, Franz 1, 2, 6, 23, 77, 80, 142
Kant, Emmanuel 9, 21, 24, 62
Kaun, Axel 17, 41
Kelly, Mr (*Murphy*) 46
Knott, Mr (*Watt*) 23, 28, 29, 31, 33, 39
Krapp 27, 63
Krapp's Last Tape 22, 24, 52, 75, 90,
    97
Lamberts (*Malone Dies*) 117
The 'laugh' 29
Lemuel (*Malone Dies*) 117
Leopardi 3
Lessness 73, 99, 100
Lindon, Jérôme 38
Locke, John 19, 42
Lords Cricket Ground 12
The Lost Ones 90, 99, 100

Luce, Dr Arthur 4
Lucilius 142
Lucky 24, 57, 60, 72–3, 94, 135
Lynch (Watt) 29
McGreevey, Thomas 129, 135
MacMann (*Malone Dies*) 117
Madden, Mr (Mercier and Camier) 87
Magdalen Mental Mercyseat 25
Magee, Patrick 90
Mahood 119
Mahoud (*The Unnamable*) 119
Malone 63, 113, 118, 121, 131
Malone Dies 36, 46, 110, 116–118, 120
Malebranche 24, 40
manicheism 24, 40
Marcos 11
Mary 111
Masson, André 80
Merlin 38–9
Mercier 51–57
Mercier and Camier 24, 28, 46
Merry Widow Waltz 97
Mihailovici, Marcel 75
Milton, John 126
Minnie (*All That Fall*) 97
Mirlittonades 29
Mohammed 112, 121
Molloy 41, 46, 49, 50, 54, 58, 63, 90,
    101, 110–118
Molloy 14, 23, 28, 32, 46, 53, 54, 116
Moll (*Malone Dies*) 117
Molly 111
Mondo Cane 11
Moore, G. E. 139–141
Moran 14, 46, 110–122
More Pricks than Kicks 5, 18, 86, 129
Moses 29, 112, 121
Mozart, W. A. 98
Murphy 5, 18, 19, 21, 22, 25, 26, 28,
    39, 43, 45, 46
Murphy 4, 16, 18, 19, 22, 23, 24, 27,
    28, 46, 86, 121
Nacht und Träume 97
Nagg (*Endgame*) 24, 57
néant 30
Nell (*Endgame*) 24, 57

Nietzsche, Friedrich 101, 121
nirvana 5, 18, 21, 26
Nixon, Richard 11
Nobel Prize 60, 132
Nohow On 102, 123
Not I 36, 101, 120
Novels of Samuel Beckett, The 145
Now the Day is over 97
O'Casey, Sean 91
Odyssey 110
Ohio Impromptu 36
Olympia Press 39
O'Neill, Eugene 91
original sin 24, 51
Orwell, George 27
Our Examination around his
    factification . . . 104, 112
Paradise Lost 126
'Perhaps' 27
Philosophical Investigations 145
Piece of Monologue 101
Pieton de l'aire 30
Pilgrim's Progress 112
Pilling, John 54, 110
Ping 99
Pinter, Harold 135
Play 35, 36, 96, 120
Pozzo (*Waiting for Godot*) 8, 9, 24,
    54, 57, 60, 71–3, 90, 135
Principia Ethica 140
Prometheus 31, 76
Prospero 103
Proust, Marcel 1, 2, 6, 17, 63–71, 73,
    77, 134, 142
*Proust and 3 Dialogues with Georges
    Duthuit* 3, 63, 129
Purgatorio 5
Rasumovsky Quartets 107
Un Regicide 66
Richard III 10
Ricks, Christopher 86
Ring der Niebelungen, Die 58
Robbe-Grillet, Alain 20, 56
Rooney, Mrs (*All That Fall*) 96
Rosebud 68
Rosset, Barney 133

Roussillion 14, 27, 114, 136
Rudmore-Brown, Thomas 4
Russell, Bertrand 9, 86
Sade, Marquis de 45, 118
Saint Bernard 93
Saint Thomas Acquinas 114
Sam (*Watt*) 40
Samuel Beckett, a Biography 146
Sapo (*Malone Dies*) 117
Saposcat (*Malone Dies*) 117
Sartre, J. P. 30, 35, 43
Schiller Theater 34
Schneider, Alan 135
Scipio 104
Schopenhauer, Arthur 6, 25, 40, 54,
    76, 95, 117, 129, 140–1
Scott, Sir Walter 13
Seaver, Richard 38
Seneca 142
Shakespeare, William 10, 89
Shaw, G. B. 55, 122
Siddhartha, Prince 14
Starkie, Walter 4
Steinbeck, John 27
Still 100
Stirrings Still 44, 102, 133
Stoics 19
Sturm und Drang 97
Surrealism 20
Sweeney Agonistes 143
Swift, Jonathon 120
Texts for Nothing 31, 101, 107, 110–1
Thatcher, Margaret 11, 139
That Time 101, 121
Thom's Dublin Directory 111
Tiberius 104
Transition 78
Trilogy (see *Molloy, Malone Dies, The
    Unnamable*) 24, 31, 39, 45, 46, 90,

    94, 98, 99, 107, 109, 111, 113, 116,
    118, 121, 137
Third New Science, The 145
Ulysses 18
The Unnamable 27, 110–111, 113,
    118–121
The Unnamable 120, 141
Ussy-sur-Marne 12, 56
Velde, Bram van 80
Vico, Giambattista 104–5
Vladimir (*Waiting for Godot*) 3, 9, 24,
    34, 35, 37, 41, 51, 53, 56, 57, 60,
    63, 68, 71, 90–1, 106–7, 119
Voltaire 1, 14
Vulture, The 42
Waiting for Godot 4, 34, 35, 39, 53, 59,
    60, 73, 90–4, 99, 101, 111–12, 116,
    135, 137
Warrilow, David 90
Watt 29, 31, 37, 38, 30–3, 37–9, 41,
    45, 46, 62, 87, 119
Watt 16, 23, 27, 28, 30
Waugh, Evelyn 27
Watt 16, 23, 27, 28, 30
The Way 145
Welles, Orson 68
What I Have Lived For (Russell) 143
What Where 38
Whoroscope 62–3
Willie (*Happy Days*) 24, 57, 58
Winnie (*Happy Days*) 24, 57, 58
Wittgenstein, Ludwig 87
Work In Progress 103
The World as Will and Representation
    142
World of the Three Rings 93
Worstward Ho 44, 102–3, 126
Yahweh (*The Unnamable*) 112, 121
Youdi (*Molloy*) 112, 113–115
Zeno's arrow 77
Zeus 76